AFTERMATH

THOMAS E. HALL

AFTERMATH

THE UNINTENDED CONSEQUENCES OF PUBLIC POLICIES

CATO
INSTITUTE
WASHINGTON, D.C.

Library of Congress Cataloging-in-Publication Data

Hall, Thomas E. (Thomas Emerson), 1954-
    Aftermath : the unintended consequences of public policies / Thomas E. Hall.
        pages cm
    Includes bibliographical references and index.
    ISBN 978-1-939709-38-7 (hardback : alk. paper) 1. Policy sciences—United
States—Case studies. 2. Political planning—United States—Case studies. 3. Income
tax—United States. 4. Cigarettes—Taxation—United States. 5. Minimum wage—
United States. 6. Prohibition—United States. I. Title.

    JK468.P64H36 2014
    320.60973--dc23

                                                                    2014017681
Printed in Canada.
Cover design: Jon Meyers

                          CATO INSTITUTE
                1000 Massachusetts Ave., N.W.
                     Washington, D.C. 20001
                          www.cato.org

To the memory of my brother Jim

Contents

List of Figures and Tables

Figures

Tables

Preface

This book describes four case studies of the law of unintended consequences as it applies to government policy. The well-known result that government policies designed to bring about one set of goals often create unanticipated outcomes has taken on increasing importance as governments become ever more involved in social and economic affairs.

I became interested in this topic while researching 20th-century U.S. macroeconomic policies. My studies of business cycles, the Great Depression (with J. D. Ferguson), and the perverse economic policies carried out during the presidencies of Richard Nixon and Jimmy Carter convinced me that most of the macroeconomic instability experienced by the United States had resulted from poorly designed government policies. I then began to consider the effects of policies targeted toward more specific issues (as opposed to the overall macroeconomy). Abundant examples of the law of unintended consequences exist; the hard part was choosing a small group to focus on.

The four cases described in this book are, I believe, interesting and important and will prove enduring. The federal income tax has existed since 1913, and given the desire of the middle and lower classes that the rich pay their "fair share," the income tax will almost certainly continue to play a major role for years to come. Cigarette taxes have been around since the 1860s and will likely be with us for as long as people smoke cigarettes. State minimum wage laws first appeared in the early 1900s, and the original federal law was put in place in 1933 as part of the New Deal. Given the ongoing demands that workers should earn a "living wage," we can expect minimum wage supporters to advocate not only for keeping the law but for continuing increases in the minimum wage. The final case is alcohol Prohibition. Although it ended in 1933 because the unintended consequences were so devastating, it has major applications to the war on drugs, which has been an explicit policy of the U.S. federal government since the early 1970s.

Several individuals assisted on this project. J. David Ferguson, D. Christopher Ferguson, William Hart, and Kenneth Ashley read drafts of chapters and offered valuable comments. I also benefited greatly from discussions with Charles Moul, James Brock, and Michael Winrow on a variety of topics. Graduate students Matt Mauck, Neel Shivdasani, and Heather McHone proofread and checked references. And my wife Christine read chapters and made comments, along with providing a loving and supportive environment. Any errors are my responsibility. Financial support for this project was provided by Miami University.

This book is dedicated to the memory of my late brother, James Ashley Hall.

1. Introduction

While driving along a residential street in the United States, you can often tell which homes are occupied by their owners and which by renters. Usually, but not always, the owner-occupied houses are better maintained, the lawns are well tended, and there is an absence of clutter on the property. Rentals often have a rougher appearance. The main reason for this difference is that owner-occupiers have a strong incentive to take care of their house and land because they live there. Absentee landlords maintain properties, but their incentive to do so is lessened somewhat since they do not occupy the premises. Tenants have even less incentive to be concerned with maintenance.

The benefits to society from homeownership are well known. In addition to the maintenance factor, owner occupiers have a greater vested interest in the well-being of their community. They are more likely to care about the quality of local schools, roads, and parks. Homeowners are also more stable residents in the sense that they move less often than renters. Also, since house prices have generally risen over time, homeownership has helped raise Americans' wealth. With these points in mind, wouldn't it be great if all American families owned their own home?

The advantages of homeownership have long been accepted in the United States, which is why the U.S. government pursues policies to promote it. This effort began in earnest during the 1930s when President Franklin Roosevelt's New Deal created various programs and agencies that encouraged homeownership: the Federal Housing Administration to insure home mortgages; the Federal National Mortgage Association (Fannie Mae) to buy mortgages insured by the Veterans Administration; the Federal Home Loan Banks to provide assistance to the savings and loan industry, which was the primary source of mortgage lending; the promotion of 30-year mortgages to lower monthly payments and make homes more affordable; the Home Owners' Loan Corporation that refinanced mortgages in default. In addition, since its inception the federal income tax code has allowed the deduction of mortgage interest from income when calculating taxes. Due in part to these various government programs, the U.S. homeownership rate, which is the proportion of U.S. houses occupied by their owners, rose from 44 percent in 1940 to 63 percent in 1970.[1]

After 1970, the growth of homeownership slowed, reaching 66 percent in 1980 before dropping back to 64 percent by the mid-1980s. It remained at that level for roughly the next 10 years. During that time, some Americans expressed concerns that homeownership was not equal across racial groups. Citing the fact that homeownership was more prevalent among whites than nonwhites, banks were accused of "redlining," an alleged practice whereby they do not issue loans to individuals or businesses in certain sections of cities. Since minorities disproportionately occupied the areas where redlining was said to be taking place, the implication was that banks were practicing discriminatory lending. This claim received support in 1992 when the Federal Reserve Bank of Boston released an influential study that reported that "black and Hispanic mortgage applicants in the Boston area were more likely to be turned down than white applicants with similar characteristics" (Munnell et al. 1992, 42).[2]

Evidence of discriminatory lending and the implication that minorities were being excluded from homeownership led to enhanced efforts by the U.S. federal government to promote home buying. In 1992, Congress passed the Housing and Community Development Act, which "essentially gave [the Federal National Mortgage Association (Fannie Mae) and the Federal Home Loan Mortgage Corporation (Freddie Mac)] a mandate to purchase lower-quality mortgages" (Acharya et al. 2011, 32). Fannie Mae and Freddie Mac are government-sponsored enterprises that purchase mortgages; after 1992, they bought increasing quantities of subprime mortgages, which are loans to higher-risk borrowers.[3] Another important factor was the 1995 amendment to the Community Reinvestment Act, which urged banks to increase lending to low-income Americans. If banks failed to meet the standards they were not subject to explicit penalties, but lending data would be made available to community groups. The implied threat was that if banks did not step up lending to minorities, then community groups would find out and organize protests and boycotts of the banks.

These laws helped create a situation that was a disaster waiting to happen. Mortgage lenders issued loans to high-risk borrowers and collected origination fees for doing so. The lenders then sold the mortgages to financial institutions, which were often Fannie Mae or Freddie Mac. If the borrowers defaulted on these mortgages, the losses would be incurred not by the original lenders but instead by the U.S. taxpayers through a government bailout of Fannie Mae and Freddie Mac, or of private banks that were also purchasing these mortgages. This ability to originate and then sell high-risk mortgages is a big reason that the absurd "no-doc" loans came into being. No-doc loans were home loans to borrowers who were not required to provide documentation of their income or assets. It is highly unlikely that such risky loans would have been made without originators being able to unload the risk onto someone else.[4]

The sorry state of affairs was made even worse by the financial industry, which was busy creating volatile financial instruments (credit derivatives) against these mortgages, and in some cases betting the institutions' fortunes on the assumption that housing prices would continue to rise. The Federal Reserve was also a big part of the problem because it maintained low interest rates during the first half of the 2000s, which encouraged Americans to borrow. Throughout that period, the government regulatory agencies in charge of monitoring the situation raised few alarms.

The expansion in mortgage lending helped raise the demand for houses, and the price increases that resulted were exceptional. Nationally, house prices rose more than 100 percent from 1995 to 2006. This large and sustained increase led to speculative buying, which further increased demand (Case and Shiller 2003). Large numbers of Americans amassed paper fortunes in real estate. The U.S. government's efforts to promote homeownership were working: the homeownership rate rose from 64 percent in 1995 to 69 percent in 2004.

However, as we know now, those policies to promote homeownership had major unanticipated effects. The housing boom eventually played out as prices peaked in 2006 and then began to decline, slowly at first, then rapidly by 2008. Falling prices caused many homeowners—especially those who had purchased their homes near the peak in prices—to owe more on their mortgage than their house was worth (a situation called "negative equity" or "underwater"). This unpleasant financial position led some homeowners to abandon the premises and stop making payments on their mortgages. In addition, when prices started to fall, fewer potential buyers saw housing as a speculative investment. Meanwhile, further pressure was placed on the housing market by the upward adjustment of interest rates on adjustable-rate mortgages issued during the boom as low introductory "teaser rates" expired. As a result of these and other factors, the demand for houses fell while the supply continued to increase (as homes being constructed during the boom were completed), causing prices to plummet. Large-scale mortgage defaults occurred, which led to losses by the financial institutions holding those mortgages. The result was the 2008 financial crisis. Since the government-sponsored enterprises Fannie Mae and Freddie Mac were heavily exposed to subprime mortgages, they were especially hard hit.

The combination of falling house prices and falling stock prices resulted in a decline of $13 trillion in U.S. household wealth, which was a major factor in causing the U.S. economy to plunge into the 2007–2009 Great Recession. This economic debacle led to the loss of 8 million jobs and the ruin of several financial institutions, including Fannie Mae and Freddie Mac, which required massive federal bailouts to stay afloat. Not surprisingly, the U.S. homeownership rate dropped, and by 2011 was back to where it had been in the late 1990s. Thus, we are left with the irony of government policies designed to promote homeownership helping cause the worst economic recession since the 1930s' Great Depression.

The 2000s' housing boom and bust is an example of the law of unintended consequences. This term refers to situations in which government policies enacted to accomplish one set of goals end up causing another set of outcomes that were unanticipated. In the case of U.S. housing policies, the federal government was attempting to achieve the honorable goal of promoting homeownership but caused an economic catastrophe while doing so. The losses to society far outweighed the gains.

How did this fiasco occur? Did the advocates of policies designed to promote homeownership not foresee the negative consequences? Or did they know there might be harmful effects but believed the benefits would outweigh the costs? Or were they aware that the adverse effects would be large but believed so strongly in their goal of promoting homeownership that they ignored the possible negative consequences?[5]

In this case, the answer appears to be that housing advocates understood that raising the homeownership rate would involve increased lending to risky borrowers, which would lead to more mortgage defaults. But housing advocates never imagined the enormous number of defaults that would occur, nor the impact that would have on the U.S. economy and financial system.

So Many Examples

There are countless examples of the law of unintended consequences as applied to government policies. One case much in the news during the last several years involves traffic cameras at street intersections. Traffic cameras have two primary purposes: (1) to motivate motorists to drive in a safe manner by not running red lights and (2) to raise revenue for local governments by allowing them to simply mail traffic tickets (along with a photo of the incident) to offending drivers. There is widespread agreement that traffic cameras raise revenue, and they may reduce the number of T-bone collisions. But there is an unintended consequence: drivers who know their actions are being recorded are much more likely to slam on the brakes to avoid running a red light. But slamming on the brakes raises the likelihood of rear-end collisions, and considerable evidence exists of this outcome taking place.[6] Since rear-end collisions are usually less injurious than T-bone collisions, traffic cameras seem justified on safety grounds, although there is disagreement on this point.

Another example is China's one-child policy, which was instituted in 1979. This policy restricts married couples to one child, although there are exceptions, depending on various factors, including the couple's ethnicity and where they live in China. Couples who violate the policy are subject to severe fines. In addition, some reports mention women enduring forced abortions and sterilizations, as well as government officials seizing babies and selling them on the adoption market. The purpose of the one-child policy is population control; on this score, it has succeeded. The Chinese government claims that the one-child policy has resulted in 400 million fewer births, although most estimates are considerably lower (Nie 2010).

This policy has also caused major unintended consequences. Since Chinese culture places a premium on baby boys, in part because males traditionally care for elderly parents, many couples strongly desire a male child. That preference has led some parents to kill their baby girls so they could try again for a boy. Accounts of widespread infanticide in China began surfacing during the 1980s. In recent years, the availability of modern technology that allows a fetus's sex to be identified has resulted in huge numbers of abortions of female fetuses. The sex ratio among children has become seriously imbalanced. For example, during 2010 in Guangdong Province, 119 baby boys were born for every 100 baby girls. A decade earlier, the ratio in that province was even worse, 130 to 100.[7]

A related consequence of the one-child policy is a shortage of marriage-age women in China. Estimates suggest that in 20 years, the ratio of Chinese marriage-age women to Chinese marriage-age men will be four to five. The problem could be solved by polygamy in the form of women with multiple husbands, but that is unlikely to happen. A much more plausible outcome is Chinese men seeking non-Chinese brides. Residents of neighboring countries are understandably nervous.

Four Case Studies

This book contains four studies of the law of unintended consequences. The discussion addresses the following questions: How did the policies come into being? Who were the advocates? What were the underlying political considerations? Why are these policies (with one exception) still in place?

The first case considered is the federal income tax and what has resulted from it. The income tax was originally instituted in 1913 for two reasons: (1) to tax high-income Americans who at the time were largely able to avoid taxes and (2) to reduce the U.S. government's financial dependence on taxes assessed on alcohol, tobacco, and imported goods, which were burdensome to middle- and low-income Americans. Thus, the establishment of the income tax was about shifting the tax burden away from the lower and middle classes and toward the upper class.

The unintended consequence was a flood of tax revenue that amazed everyone, including the income tax's creators. These funds allowed politicians, who can rarely resist the temptation to spend every cent of available revenue and then some, to go on a spending spree that has lasted decades. The federal income tax is a major reason why we have the huge federal government we live with today, one that is several orders of magnitude larger than the Founding Fathers ever imagined.

Cigarette taxes are examined next. These taxes are collected by the U.S. federal government, along with all 50 states and the District of Columbia, and some counties and cities. They were originally imposed solely as a revenue source for governments, and they have been very effective in that regard because tobacco is an addictive substance. Since the 1960s when the link between smoking and health problems was documented, an additional justification has been on health grounds: taxing cigarettes discourages smoking, which results in a healthier population. More recently, as governments have increasingly funded health care, cigarette taxes have been rationalized on the grounds that the revenue is needed to help pay the higher health care costs incurred by smokers.

The major unintended consequence of cigarette taxes is the criminal activity they create. Large differences in tax rates across jurisdictions present criminals with a profit opportunity: they can purchase cigarettes in low-tax areas and then illegally transport them to high-tax areas where they are sold. Cigarette smuggling is a huge business in the United States and is largely controlled by organized crime syndicates. Most Americans are aware that it takes place but are unaware of its magnitude. Since many states seem intent on raising cigarette taxes to ever-greater heights, this smuggling problem will not only persist, it will worsen.

The third case is the U.S. minimum wage law. Minimum wage laws first appeared at the state level in the early 1900s and were advocated as a method of raising the cost of employing women and children so that employers would replace them with adult men. Several additional arguments were used to justify these laws, such as ensuring that workers earned enough to afford a decent standard of living (i.e., a "living wage") and encouraging children to attend school instead of working. The federal minimum wage law was enacted in the 1930s and has existed ever since.

The problem with a minimum wage law is that it can artificially raise the wage rate of marginal workers above the value they create while working for an hour. If that occurs, businesses will employ fewer of these low-skill workers, replacing some of them with machines, or altering business practices to save labor. So at a basic level, the minimum wage is about a choice: (1) a smaller number of workers earning a higher legally mandated minimum wage or (2) a larger number of workers earning a lower market-determined wage. Most economists would argue in favor of the latter, yet society chooses the former. One major reason that this law has survived is that the beneficiaries of minimum wage laws tend to be adults, while the losers are often teenagers. Another consideration is that the losers (those who are unemployed because of the law) are harder to identify than the winners (which include those with jobs at the minimum wage).

The final case is alcohol Prohibition, which existed from 1920 to 1933. The unintended negative consequences of Prohibition were so obvious and enormous that the policy was eventually abandoned. The intent was to reduce alcohol consumption, which the Prohibition laws accomplished, although by nowhere nearly as much as the proponents originally predicted. The basic problem was that the law's intent was easily bypassed through both legal and illegal means. Illegal alcohol was the main factor in causing Prohibition's undoing, as criminal gangs became major players in the U.S. alcoholic beverage industry. They produced and sold so much poisoned booze that tens of thousands of Americans died and many more were sickened. Prohibition also led to soaring levels of corruption by public officials and caused a major crime wave that filled America's courts and prisons to capacity and beyond. After experiencing these problems for several years, Americans finally said "enough" and ended Prohibition.

The moral of these stories is that whenever you hear about a new government policy being considered, give thought to potential unintended consequences. Policies created for one set of purposes almost always create an additional set of results that were not part of the original plan. Very often these unintended consequences are seriously adverse.

2. Federal Income Taxes: Funding the Welfare State

The Congress shall have the power to lay and collect taxes on incomes, from whatever source derived, without apportionment among the several States, and without regard to any census or enumeration.

—Sixteenth Amendment to the U.S. Constitution, ratified February 3, 1913

The seeds of today's big-government welfare state were sown during the post–Civil War industrial boom in the United States. Industrialization caused the gap between America's rich and working-class families to widen, and that growing income disparity was instrumental in creating popular support for a federal income tax. Motivated by a sense of social justice, many Americans, especially western and southern farmers, hammered by the effects of financial crises and deflation during the late 1800s, came to believe that the government should tax the income and wealth of the upper class. A small number of business-owning families had become phenomenally wealthy after the Civil War, and the public resented their political influence, as well as their anti-competitive business behavior, which was viewed as being responsible for the high prices U.S. consumers paid for finished goods. In addition, the financial manipulations of these business tycoons were considered a primary cause of the periodic financial crises that plagued the nation.

The U.S. tax system in place at the time allowed the super-rich to accumulate and retain their fortunes while avoiding major tax burdens. State and local governments relied primarily on property taxes for their revenue, and most wealthy industrialists were not large landowners. The federal government collected the bulk of its revenue from taxes on imported goods (called tariffs, or customs duties), along with excise taxes on tobacco and alcohol. Although upper-class Americans paid those taxes, they did so in amounts that were nowhere nearly as large a proportion of their incomes as was the case for ordinary Americans. Wealthy capitalists earned their incomes as profits from businesses they owned, and that income was not taxed. Another important source of

9

their income was interest earned on bank accounts and bonds, and that wasn't taxed either. So the super-rich families of the era were able to earn essentially tax-free incomes that middle- and lower-class Americans believed were being earned at their expense. It was a situation rife for creating resentment.

Americans vented their frustration with this state of affairs by supporting a federal tax on personal incomes and corporate profits. That tax came about in 1894 when Congress imposed a 2 percent tax on incomes above $4,000, a very high income at that time. However, in 1895 the U.S. Supreme Court declared the tax unconstitutional on the grounds that it was a "direct tax" that, according to the U.S. Constitution, had to be apportioned among the individual states based on their populations. Thus, the 1894 income tax suffered a quick death and by doing so made its supporters realize that a permanent income tax would require a constitutional amendment. The effort to bring that about took place during the early 1900s and eventually resulted in the Sixteenth Amendment, which was ratified in 1913.

The great irony of the U.S. federal income tax is that the original supporters apparently gave little thought to what to do with the revenue it would generate other than to use it to reduce the federal government's dependence on tariffs and excise taxes as funding sources. This lack of foresight likely occurred because income tax advocates had no idea how much revenue the tax would actually bring in. In fact, what happened was the income tax—originally created to shift the tax burden away from the middle and lower classes and toward the upper-class capitalists—turned out to be the mother of all cash cows. It brought in unprecedented amounts of revenue, and by doing so had the unintended consequence of allowing the enormous expansion of the federal government. The income tax was instrumental in helping create the huge federal bureaucracy that many Americans complain about today.

Rise of the Super-rich

In 1789, the upper strata of American society consisted of landowners in the South and merchants who were primarily located in the North. For example, Virginians George Washington and Thomas Jefferson were wealthy because they owned large amounts of property in the form of land and slaves, and they earned their incomes primarily from selling crops produced by that property. Wealthy landowners paid property taxes, and those taxes were the major source of revenue to state governments at the time.[1]

The merchants earned their incomes from exporting goods produced in North America, such as tobacco and rum, and importing finished goods and slaves. These merchants paid tariffs, or customs duties, on imported goods, and that revenue was the primary source of funds for the federal government. The government collected tariffs from the merchants, but consumers actually paid the tariffs in the form of higher prices for the imported goods.

This system of taxation was essentially unchanged until the Civil War (1861–1865). When the conflict erupted, the government needed additional revenue to finance the U.S. military effort. So Congress passed several tax laws that raised tariffs; increased excise taxes on many products, including alcohol and tobacco; and imposed the nation's first federal income tax. The public was amenable to these taxes because they supported the war. But when the war ended, the taxes were no longer viewed as necessary, so Congress eliminated many of them, including the income tax. It retained the higher tariffs on imports and the excise taxes on alcohol and tobacco. The federal government was once again largely dependent on import tariffs and excise taxes on alcohol and tobacco for revenue. States continued to rely on property taxes.

The rise of the capitalists during the post–Civil War era changed the composition of America's elite by replacing landowners and merchants with business owners, such as Andrew Carnegie (steel), John D. Rockefeller (oil), J. P. Morgan (banking), and Philip Armour (meat packing). These capitalists owned land and paid property taxes, but those taxes were not a major consideration to them. Tariffs were not a burden either; in fact, many industrialists benefited enormously from import taxes because they offered protection from foreign import competition. So the capitalist business tycoons had an incredible deal: they were able to accumulate unprecedented amounts of income and wealth, largely free of taxes, and were made even richer by the protective tariff that was primarily paid by the middle class.

Vast fortunes allowed the upper class to enjoy lifestyles that were mind-boggling by the standards of the day: multiple mansions, scores of servants, yachts, private railcars, fabulous collections of art and jewelry, grand tours of Europe. A social observer of the era reports that "in the mansion of the genteel captain of industry there must be five or six servants to receive you, as well as a butler. The butler and three servants in livery served you dinner. . . . To serve a cup of tea two servants were necessary" (Josephson 1934, 334). Many of the United States' so-called 400 richest families led lives similar to European royalty, something that did not go over well with many citizens of the democratic United States.

As the industrial boom continued, public resentment built up against both the wealthy capitalists and the U.S. system of taxation. Farmers, who dominated the politics of western and southern states, accumulated a long list of grievances. They were increasingly bitter over their belief that they paid more than their share of the tax burden. They resented the protective tariff that lined the pockets of the industrialists by caus- ing the high prices the farmers paid for finished goods. They were being decimated by bouts of farm price deflation that occurred during the fre- quent economic recessions. Farmers attributed these business downturns to financial machinations of eastern capitalists, such as the 1873 crisis set off by the failure of Philadelphia financier Jay Cooke's bank. Farmers also abhorred the gold standard, the monetary system in place that was blamed for the deflation taking place during the era. The gold standard was widely supported by eastern manufacturing and financial interests who valued "sound money." Southerners had an additional item on their list of complaints: federal tax revenue was being used to pay increasingly generous pensions to Union army veterans and their families. By the late 1890s, those pensions consumed as much as 45 percent of federal revenue (Brownlee 1996, 31). Former Confederates paid taxes to support those pensions but, of course, did not receive them.

As a result of these and other factors, the Republicans experienced a gradual erosion of political rule. The Democrats, who had western and southern support, won control of the House of Representatives in the 1874 elections and the Senate in 1878. During the ensuing years, Demo- crats and Republicans traded power back and forth. But when Demo- crat Grover Cleveland was sworn in for his second term as president (1893–1897), the Democrats held both houses of Congress. Now was their big chance to enact the United States' first peacetime income tax.

Early Federal Income Taxes

As noted earlier, the first federal income tax was imposed in 1861 to help pay for the Civil War. Viewed as temporary (it expired in 1872), the tax was designed to collect revenue from high-income earners. It exempted the first $800 of income (later lowered to $600) at a time when a typical worker earned about $300 per year. Tax rates were altered twice, varying from 3 percent to 10 percent.[2] During the war, the tax provided about 25 percent of federal revenue.[3] As an indicator of where high-income earners lived at the time, well over half of the income tax's revenue was paid by residents and businesses located in New York, Pennsylvania, and Massachusetts (Selig- man 1914, 472). Prosperous New York, with roughly 17 percent of the U.S. population, paid 33 percent of U.S. federal income taxes.

When the Democrats resurrected the income tax in 1894, it had strong public support. Included as part of a tariff bill, the first $4,000 of income from all sources, including dividends and interest, was exempted, and income above that amount was taxed at a rate of 2 percent. During congressional debate on the bill, northeastern politicians were opposed, in part because they were aware that their constituents would pay most of the tax. Supporters framed the debate as rich versus poor, where the rich should pay their fair share. Opponents countered that an income tax was a socialistic seizure of property. The bill passed Congress and became law in August 1894.

The following year, a court case involving the income tax was argued before the U.S. Supreme Court. The major issue was whether the income tax was a "direct" tax. If so, then the U.S. Constitution clearly states that it must be apportioned based on states' populations. In other words, if New York had twice the population of Georgia, then total taxes collected from residents and businesses in New York should be two times the amount collected from Georgia. But at the time, with so much of the nation's financial wealth and income concentrated in New York, a tax on high-income earners would cause total taxes paid by New Yorkers to be far more than twice the amount paid by all residents and businesses in Georgia. Thus, the tax would not be apportioned according to the two states' populations, which would violate the Constitution's clause on direct taxes.

It is not exactly clear what the Framers of the U.S. Constitution meant by the term "direct tax" because many of those involved in writing and ratifying the document had different things in mind. But the term became interpreted in constitutional law as meaning a tax on property or a head tax (an identical tax imposed on each person). The issue in the court case hinged on the following: a tax *on property* is clearly a direct tax, but what about a tax *on the income earned from property*?[4] Is that a direct tax or an indirect tax? If it was a direct tax, then the 1894 income tax law was unconstitutional; but if it was an indirect tax, then it would be constitutional and not subject to the clause about apportionment based on states' populations. This issue never came up while the Civil War income tax was in effect, apparently because the members of Congress thought it was an indirect tax.

In a decision that set off a major legal debate that lasted years, the U.S. Supreme Court ruled in 1895 that the income tax assessed on income derived from land was a direct tax.[5] Thus, the 1894 income tax law was ruled unconstitutional. Following a rehearing on the case, the Court later stated that taxing income earned on personal property (which includes assets such as stocks and bonds) was a direct tax. Income tax proponents were devastated by these rulings because they meant that the creation of a lasting income tax law would require a constitutional amendment that could take years to bring about.

That effort did take years, in part because the nation's focus shifted to the debate over the gold standard, which was the major issue in the hotly contested 1896 national election. During his campaign, Democratic presidential candidate William Jennings Bryan made his famous "Cross of Gold" speech, claiming that farmers were being crucified by the gold standard and the deflation it caused. The Republicans and their candidate William McKinley firmly backed the gold standard. It was East and Midwest versus West and South, and McKinley won a close race while congressional Republicans managed to retain their majorities in both the House and Senate. With the Republicans in control, the gold standard was retained and the income tax was moved to the back burner. Yet public support for an income tax continued.

Moving toward a Constitutional Amendment

The protective tariff was another major political issue during the late 1800s and early 1900s. Westerners and southerners continued to blame tariffs for high finished-goods prices, thereby making eastern capitalists wealthy at their expense. At the same time, many Americans, regardless of where they lived, believed that corporations and wealthy Americans should pay income taxes. President Theodore Roosevelt, who occupied the White House from 1901 to 1909, never advocated tariff reform, but in 1906 he did come out in support of an income tax.

Three years later, incoming president William Howard Taft pressed the Republican Congress to modify the tariff law, and the result was the 1909 Payne-Aldrich Tariff Act. Passed after a frenzy of lobbying by various manufacturing groups, the bill lowered tariff rates on some items, but in many cases they were goods that were not imported, or imported only in small quantities. Meanwhile, well over half the tariffs were raised. Congress had hardly "reformed" the law, and everyone knew it. In disgust, a group of congressional Republicans split from their party and aligned themselves with the Democrats. President Taft tried to defuse the party revolt by coming out in support of a corporate profits tax and recommending that Congress approve a constitutional amendment making an income tax possible. These bills passed Congress, apparently because many Republicans in the House and Senate viewed them as the political cost of keeping the protective tariff in place (Carson 1977, 78–80).[6]

The proposed amendment would give Congress the authority to impose an income tax that was not apportioned among the states according to population. In 1909, Congress approved the following and sent it to the states for ratification:

> The Congress shall have the power to lay and collect taxes on incomes, from whatever source derived, without apportionment among the several States, and without regard to any census or enumeration.

Many have speculated about whether the Republicans actually wanted the states to ratify the amendment, contending that it was political cover for the upcoming 1910 congressional elections. If so, the strategy failed miserably, because the Republicans lost the House in 1910 and the Senate in 1912. Also in 1912, Theodore Roosevelt ran for president as a third-party candidate, which split the Republican vote and allowed Democrat Woodrow Wilson to emerge victorious. Once again, the Democrats controlled both the federal executive and legislative branches.

The Amendment Passes

Garnering considerably more support in the East than contemporary observers predicted, the Sixteenth Amendment was ratified on February 3, 1913. President Wilson was inaugurated in March, and during the summer Congress debated an income tax law that was ultimately included in the Underwood Tariff Act. Tariff rates were dropped to their lowest levels since before the Civil War. The new income tax was supposed to make up for the lost tariff revenue, and this part of the bill was short and simple, taking up only 14 pages of U.S. law. The four-page tax form (including instructions) defined income as coming from several sources, including wages, dividends, interest, business profits, and capital gains. It allowed deductions for expenses, including interest, taxes, casualty losses, depreciation, and uncollectible debt. All information was self-reported, and after determining net income, the following tax table applied for married couples:

Income	Tax Rate
$0–$3,999	0%
$4,000–$20,000	1%
$20,001–$50,000	2%
$50,001–$75,000	3%
$75,001–$100,000	4%
$100,001–$250,000	5%
$250,001–$500,000	6%
Greater than $500,000	7%

Source: www.irs.gov/pub/irs-utl/1913.pdf.

At the time, a middle-class family earned an annual income of around $500–$700 per year, so the vast majority of Americans were exempt from the tax.[7] Largely for this reason, the arrival of the personal income tax was greeted with little public fanfare.

More Revenue Needed

The first tax returns were filed in the spring of 1914, and just a few months later World War I began in Europe. Initially, most Americans wanted no part of the conflict, but attitudes changed in 1915 when the German navy torpedoed the passenger ship *Lusitania*, killing 1,198 people, of whom 139 were Americans. This event inflamed anti-German feelings in the United States, and the U.S. federal government responded by increasing expenditures on defense goods. By 1916, higher defense spending combined with falling revenue from customs duties (due to fewer imports from war-torn Europe) caused the government to incur a sizable budget deficit. More revenue was needed, and the income tax was suddenly, conveniently available.

The Emergency Revenue Act of 1916 raised the tax rate on incomes above $4,000 from 1 percent to 2 percent, and pushed the top rate to 13 percent on incomes above $2 million. Several other taxes were also raised, including excise taxes on alcohol and tobacco and taxes on the profits of war munitions manufacturers. In addition, a federal inheritance tax was imposed. However, the deficit continued to expand because of the ongoing military buildup. So Congress raised rates again in 1917, just months before the United States finally declared war. The War Revenue Act of 1917 lowered the tax-exempt income level from $4,000 to $2,000 for a married couple and established tax brackets that ranged from a tax rate of 2 percent to 50 percent on incomes over $1 million. In addition, tax rates were increased on corporate profits and inheritances, and several excise taxes were raised.

The 1917 War Revenue Act was a significant event because, as Witte notes, "the crucial result was the discovery of how easily and quickly large sums of revenue could be raised through the income taxes" (1985, 81). The next year another Revenue Act (1918) was passed that returned the exempt income amount back to $4,000, but elevated the bottom tax rate to 12 percent and the top rate to 77 percent on incomes above $1 million. Higher tax rates in conjunction with the booming war economy caused federal revenue to soar. Here are federal revenue data from 1915 to 1920:

Year	Revenue (millions)
1915	$683
1916	$761

1917	$1,100
1918	$3,645
1919	$5,130
1920	$6,648

Source: U.S. Bureau of the Census (1975, 1106).

During these years, taxes on individual incomes and corporate profits accounted for about two-thirds of total revenue (Faulkner 1960, 598). The top rates were now punitive, a fact recognized by both President Wilson and Treasury Secretary Carter Glass. They believed that high tax rates could have an adverse affect on economic activity by reducing the incentive to earn income (Witte 1985, 88).

In summary, World War I was a very important event in the history of the U.S. income tax because it starkly demonstrated the income tax's ability to raise major amounts of revenue quickly. In addition, it marked the first time the government instituted punitive tax rates. It was also the era when the income tax replaced excise taxes on tobacco and alcohol as the major source of federal revenue.[8]

Changing of the Guard

World War I and its aftermath cost the Democrats dearly in the 1918 and 1920 elections. They lost control of Congress in the 1918 elections, and incurred further damage by losing more congressional seats along with the White House in 1920. The Republicans assumed control of the government in March 1921 and held power for the remainder of the decade.

A major economic policy figure during the 1920s was Pittsburgh industrialist Andrew Mellon, who served as U.S. treasury secretary from 1921 to 1932. Mellon agreed with Woodrow Wilson's and Carter Glass's claim that high income tax rates reduced the incentive to earn taxable income, but Mellon took the argument a step further. He believed that if the disincentive to earn income was strong enough, then high tax rates could yield less revenue than if rates were lower. In other words, lowering income tax rates might cause people to earn enough additional income to cause an increase in tax revenue. This view was an important part of Mellon's case about why income tax rates should be reduced, and congressional Republicans and Presidents Warren Harding and Calvin Coolidge were amenable to it.

The result was a series of tax laws passed during the 1920s that reduced income tax rates, including lowering the top rate from 73 percent to 24 percent. Many economists consider these lower tax rates to be one of the reasons that the U.S. economy performed so well during the decade. The income tax was also made more broadly based by reducing the income exemption so as to raise the number of taxpayers (although the tax was still directed at high incomes). In the early 1920s, the income exemption for married couples was reduced from $4,000 to $2,500.[9] Given the tremendous economic growth that took place during the decade (per capita income rose about 30 percent from 1920 to 1929), ever-increasing numbers of Americans paid taxes.[10]

Meanwhile, the federal government was shrinking in relation to the overall economy. In 1920, federal outlays were $6.6 billion, which represented 7.3 percent of that year's economic output. By 1929, federal outlays were $3.8 billion, or 3.5 percent of economic output.[11]

Raising Taxes during the Depression

The Great Depression (1929–1941) ranks among the most significant events ever to occur in the United States. The severity of the initial economic recession (1929–1933) is important to the history of the income tax because it caused plummeting incomes, which resulted in a huge decline in tax revenue. Consequently, the federal government experienced sizable budget deficits. The prevailing view at the time was that budget deficits should be avoided, and one way to balance the budget was to raise revenue. Mellon's idea that lower tax rates could yield more revenue was thrown out the window. The government instead opted for higher tax rates.

President Herbert Hoover started the tax increase ball rolling in 1932. Figure 2.1 shows the top and bottom federal income tax rates from 1913 to 2011. The budget deficit was a major issue in the 1932 presidential election between incumbent Herbert Hoover and challenger Franklin Roosevelt, and both men pledged to balance the budget. In 1932, before the election, Hoover supported higher tax rates as a way to raise revenue, and Congress passed the tax increase in June. Figure 2.1 shows that tax rates rose substantially for high-income taxpayers as the top rate went from 24 percent to 63 percent. The corporate profit tax rate was increased as well. These higher tax rates, however, did not eliminate the budget deficit because the economy continued to plunge in 1932, in part because the higher tax rates reduced both spending and the incentive to earn income.

The 1929–1933 recession had a huge impact on the fortunes of the country's two major political parties. The Republicans went from enjoying substantial congressional majorities in the late 1920s to very thin margins (one seat in the Senate, two in the House) following the 1930 elections. The coup de grâce came in 1932, when the Democrats gained 12 Senate seats and nearly 100 House seats. The Democrats also won the presidency that year when Franklin Roosevelt scored a landslide victory over

Figure 2.1
TOP AND BOTTOM FEDERAL MARGINAL TAX RATES ON INCOME, 1913–2011

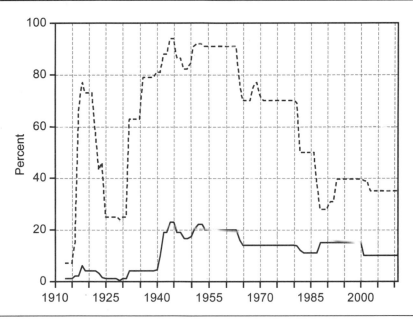

SOURCES: 1913–2002, IRS, www.irs.gov; 2003–2011, Tax Foundation, www.tax foundation.org.

Hoover. The incoming president's plans for economic stimulus included various New Deal programs for work relief and welfare that would require significant funding. Since the government's budget was already in deficit and Roosevelt intended to spend even more, the plan was to raise tax rates to generate additional revenue. The public, many of whom blamed the Great Depression on a failure of capitalism, supported higher taxes so long as the increases were targeted at the upper-class capitalists.

Figure 2.2 shows federal revenue and spending data from 1929 to 1940. Roosevelt's New Deal began in March 1933, and during the next few years, the programs required ever more funds. The economic recovery combined with the higher income tax rates that took effect in 1932 caused revenue to rise, but not fast enough to eliminate the federal budget deficit. So beginning in 1934, Congress passed and President Roosevelt signed a series of tax laws that substantially raised rates on personal income, corporate income, and inheritances. For example, the 1936

Figure 2.2
FEDERAL RECEIPTS, SPENDING, AND BUDGET SURPLUS, 1929–1940

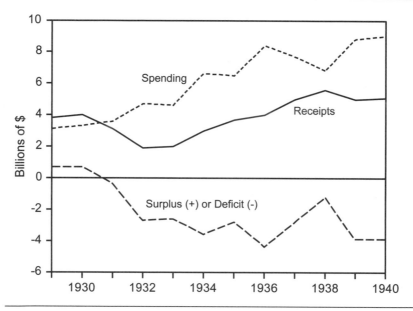

SOURCE: Economic Report of the President (1963, p. 238). Data are for fiscal year July 1–June 30.

Revenue Act maintained the $2,500 exemption for a married couple, but raised tax rates to a maximum of 79 percent on incomes above $5 million. Corporate income was taxed at a maximum rate of 15 percent, plus a tax was instituted on undistributed profits. Francois Velde estimates that for households earning more than $4,000, this law nearly doubled the average tax rate from 6.4 percent to 11.6 percent (2009, 19). Another major tax change during the decade was the institution of the Social Security tax in 1937.[12] The Social Security Act (1935) imposed a 2 percent payroll tax on the first $3,000 of wage income beginning in 1937. That year, the new tax accounted for 10.5 percent of federal tax revenue (Velde 2009, 19).[13]

Except for the Social Security levy, taxes assessed on income during the Depression were directed at high earners. This feature of the tax laws provided the upper class with a strong incentive to avoid paying taxes. After all, these income tax increases were not temporary war-funding measures; instead they were peacetime measures that might be in place for a long time. Wealthy Americans—some of whom considered Roosevelt (who was descended from an upper-class New York family) a "traitor to his class"—hired lawyers and accountants to figure out ways to avoid paying.[14] For example, business owners could compensate themselves in the form of nontaxable fringe benefits instead of taxable wages and business profits. Corporations did similar sorts of things; one common method was to move operations offshore to avoid paying taxes. During congressional hearings in 1937, members of Congress were shown photographs of small shacks on Caribbean islands that served as corporate headquarters for tax purposes (Carson 1977, 120).

High tax rates also increased the opportunity for politicians to hand out more political favors in the form of tax breaks. Taxpayers subject to high rates had a strong incentive to appeal to their political representatives for relief. Members of Congress were able to hand out benefits in the form of tax exemptions for various activities, the implied quid pro quo being that the beneficiaries would lend political support and campaign contributions to their representatives and senators. Such an arrangement is less likely to occur if tax rates are low because income earners have a smaller incentive to avoid taxes.

When World War II broke out in Europe in 1939, President Roosevelt was concerned that the conflict would eventually engulf the United States. So he pushed for additional taxes to fund a military buildup. Rates were raised again in 1940, and that year the exempt amount for a married couple was lowered to $2,000. Then in 1941, the married exemption was lowered to $1,500, and the bottom tax rate was raised from 4 percent to 10 percent. The middle class was now paying federal income taxes.

World War II

Funding the enormous U.S. military effort during World War II led to a major expansion of the income tax. Just days after the December 7, 1941, Japanese attack on Pearl Harbor, the United States was formally at war with Japan, Germany, and Italy. And it was painfully clear to Americans that carrying out military operations in both Europe and the Pacific would require an enormous amount of physical and financial resources. There was considerable discussion about how this undertaking would be financed, and the Roosevelt administration decided that taxes would play an important role.

The income tax law was altered in 1942 to capture even more income earners. The marriage exemption was lowered to $1,200; for single earners, the amount was $624. Tax rates were raised again, the bottom rate to 19 percent and the top rate to 88 percent (on incomes above $200,000). This huge tax increase was initiated to help support the war effort: more

21

income earners would now pay taxes, and those already paying would be subject to substantially higher rates. President Roosevelt hailed the new law as "the greatest tax bill in American history."[15] The following year, payroll withholding was instituted; this is the system under which income taxes are withheld from paychecks throughout the year. Previously, taxpayers paid their entire tax bill when filing their returns.

As was the case during World War I—only this time on a much larger scale—the combination of the lower income exemption, the higher tax rates, and the booming war economy caused both the number of taxpayers and taxes paid to soar. During fiscal year 1939, 7.5 million income tax returns were filed and $890 million was collected in taxes. In 1945, 49.9 million returns were filed and $17 billion in income taxes were collected (U.S. Bureau of the Census 1975, 1110). Corporate income taxes (including the tax on "excess profits") also soared by a similar order of magnitude, from $1.2 billion in 1939 to $14.9 billion in 1944 (U.S. Bureau of the Census 1975, 1109). However, despite this surge in revenue, it was not enough to keep pace with wartime expenditures. From 1942 to 1945, the federal government incurred budget deficits totaling $184 billion (Council of Economic Advisers 1962, 207, 272).[16] During World War II, tax revenue funded about 45 percent of U.S. federal expenditures (R. A. Gordon 1974, 85).[17]

The Postwar Era and the Cold War

At the conclusion of prior U.S. military conflicts, the federal government reduced defense spending and lowered tax rates. This process took place after World War II, but to a lesser extent than had been the case before. Beginning in 1945, the federal government downsized but remained larger than it had been just before the war, and much larger than before the Great Depression. This expanded government was partly because the New Deal had created several permanent federal spending programs and regulatory agencies. The other major cause was change on the international political scene.

When World War II ended, the Soviet Union's Red Army occupied Eastern Europe. As a counterweight to the communist threat, the United States maintained military bases in Western and Southern Europe. The United States also maintained a presence in the Pacific, with bases in various locations, including Japan and Okinawa. U.S. concerns over communist aggression proved correct when in 1949 the Soviets cut off West Berlin from West Germany, which precipitated the Berlin Airlift. Also that year, the communists won the Chinese civil war. The following year, the North Korean communists attacked South Korea, which ignited the Korean War. The Cold War was on, and it would require a permanently large U.S. military.

Table 2.1 contains data on federal employment, both total employees and the number of federal workers employed in national defense. In 1929, the U.S. federal government employed 579,500 workers, and during the Great Depression, the number expanded because of the New Deal programs. Defense employment grew slightly faster than overall federal employment, rising from 18 to 21 percent of federal employment. World War II caused a surge in the number of federal employees, largely for defense. At the war's end in 1945, the federal government had 2.6 million defense workers, the vast majority of them in uniform, which constituted 69 percent of all federal employees. The military was then reduced, but by 1949 it still accounted for 42 percent of federal employment. During the Korean War (1950–1953), defense employment expanded to about 50 percent of federal workers, then remained above 40 percent during the ensuing Cold War era.

Table 2.1
FEDERAL EMPLOYMENT IN SELECTED YEARS, 1929–1964
(THOUSANDS OF PAID EMPLOYEES)

Year	Federal Employment	Federal Defense Employment	Defense as % of Total
1929	579.5	103.1	18
1933	603.6	101.2	17
New Deal			
1934	698.6	133.1	19
1939	953.9	196.0	21
World War II			
1941	1,437.7	556.1	39
1942	2,296.4	1,291.1	56
1945	3,816.3	2,634.6	69
Post WWII			
1949	2,102.1	879.9	42
Korean War			
1951	2,482.7	1,235.5	50
1953	2,558.4	1,332.1	52
Post Korean War to Pre-Vietnam War			
1958	2,382.5	1,097.1	46
1960	2,398.7	1,047.1	44
1964	2,500.5	1,029.8	41

SOURCE: U.S Bureau of the Census (1975, p. 1102).

The permanently larger government provided a reason to maintain the World War II tax rates, although the Republicans did try to lower them. They took control of Congress after the 1946 elections and promptly passed tax rate reductions. But President Truman vetoed these changes, citing as his reasons the budget deficit and concerns that unemployment and inflation would rise after the war (Witte 1985, 131–44). Congress was unable to override his veto. By 1948, however, a postwar depression had not appeared, and the federal government was running a budget surplus. With two of Truman's reasons no longer valid, congressional Republicans were able to attract enough Democratic votes to override another Truman veto and enact a modest tax reduction.

Despite these reductions, tax rates were still much higher than they had been during the 1920s. These higher rates, combined with the expanding postwar U.S. economy, provided the funding for another major expansion of the federal government.

The Growth of Transfer Payments

Figure 2.3 shows U.S. federal outlays from 1929 to 2009. The series that excludes transfer payments (the dotted line) consists of outlays for defense, the post office, foreign affairs, general government, and spending on infrastructure (roads, harbors, airports, etc.). The solid line includes transfer payments, which are primarily Social Security and Medicare benefits, but also federal poverty programs (including Medicaid) and interest on the debt.

As Figure 2.3 makes clear, the major growth in federal spending during the past several decades has been in transfer payments, which reflects the rise of the welfare state. The two series diverged in the 1950s, and the gap continued to widen during the decades that followed. Major sources of transfer payments' growth have been Medicare and Medicaid, both created in 1965, and Social Security benefits, which became more generous during the 1960s and 1970s. More recently, increased numbers of retiring baby boomers (with millions more in the pipeline) have led to further expansion of transfer payments.

The data plotted in Figure 2.3 are not adjusted for inflation, nor do they account for the fact that the U.S. economy has expanded over time. Figure 2.4 makes these adjustments by plotting federal outlays as a proportion of annual U.S. gross domestic product (GDP), which is the standard measure of the nation's economic output. In 1929, federal spending was 2.7 percent of GDP, of which 1.6 percentage points were transfer payments. The 1930s' New Deal programs caused these values to rise, and then during World War II, the government soared in size, peaking at almost 50 percent

Figure 2.3
FEDERAL GOVERNMENT OUTLAYS INCLUDING AND EXCLUDING TRANSFER PAYMENTS, NOMINAL VALUES, 1929–2009

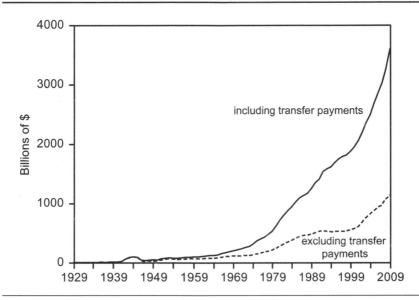

SOURCE: Federal Reserve Bank of St. Louis, FRED data set.

of economic output in 1944 and 1945. Transfer payments began diverging from the other outlays after the Korean War. Since then, federal spending excluding transfer payments has declined relative to economic output; in fact, the series is now roughly where it was in the late 1940s. Meanwhile, transfer payments rose to nearly 12 percent of GDP by the mid-2000s.

Table 2.2 shows various components of federal receipts and outlays during two recent years. In 2007, federal receipts were 19.4 percent of GDP, with the individual income tax accounting for 8.8 percentage points and the Social Security and Medicare taxes comprising 6.6 percentage points. That same year federal outlays for transfer payments—Medicare, Social Security, income security, and net interest—were 11.8 percent of GDP. The 2007–2009 recession caused tax receipts to decline relative to income, to 16.2 percent of GDP by 2010. Meanwhile, a federal spending binge caused outlays to expand to 25.8 percent of GDP, of which 14.8 percentage points were transfer payments. Since receipts were 16.2 percent of GDP while outlays were 25.8 percent, the government borrowed the difference (9.6 percentage points of GDP).

Figure 2.4
FEDERAL GOVERNMENT OUTLAYS INCLUDING AND EXCLUDING
TRANSFER PAYMENTS, AS PERCENT OF GROSS DOMESTIC PRODUCT,
1929–2009

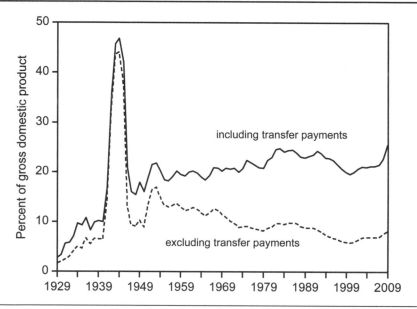

SOURCE: Federal Reserve Bank of St. Louis, FRED data set.

In other words, in 2010 the federal government collected about 16 cents of every dollar of income produced in the United States, and spent 25 cents (of which 15 cents were transfer payments). This shortfall required federal borrowing of almost 10 percent of GDP produced that year. The federal government has evolved into a monolith that taxes "Peter" (those with jobs or earning high incomes, or both) to pay "Paul" (primarily senior citizens receiving Social Security and Medicare benefits). In effect, this is an intergenerational transfer scheme that taxes workers and pays older retirees. Retirees, of course, feel entitled to these benefits because they have paid taxes into this system while they worked, and the current workers accept the arrangement so long as they believe benefits will be available when they retire.

The huge expansion of transfer payments has required higher tax rates to help fund them. Recall that in 1937, the original Social Security payroll tax rate for OASDI (old-age, survivors, and disability insurance)

Table 2.2
FEDERAL RECEIPTS AND OUTLAYS AS PERCENT OF GROSS DOMESTIC PRODUCT, 2007 AND 2010

	Receipts				
Year	Total Receipts (%)	Individual Income Tax (%)	Corporate Income Tax (%)	Social Security & Medicare Tax (%)	Other*
2007	19.4	8.8	2.8	6.6	1.2
2010	16.2	6.7	1.4	6.5	1.6

*Other receipts include gift and estate taxes, excise taxes, customs duties, and Federal Reserve deposits.

	Outlays						
Year	Total Outlays (%)	Defense (%)	Medi-care (%)	Social Security (%)	Income Security (%)	Net Interest (%)	Other**
2007	20.6	4.2	2.8	4.4	2.8	1.8	4.7
2010	25.8	5.2	3.4	5.3	4.6	1.5	5.8

**Other outlays include international affairs, health, and post office.

	Federal Deficit
Year	
2007	1.2
2010	9.6

SOURCE: Federal Reserve Bank of St. Louis, FRED data set.

was 2 percent. Figure 2.5 shows the payroll tax rates for OASDI and Medicare hospitalization insurance.[18] The Social Security tax has risen more than sixfold (from 2.0 percent to 12.4 percent), whereas the Medicare tax went from 0.7 percent when first instituted in 1966 to the current rate of 2.9 percent. Another difference between the two levies is that the Social Security tax has an annual income limit beyond which the wage earner pays no further taxes (in 2010, the amount was $106,800), whereas the Medicare tax has no income limit.

Our Modern Federal Tax System

In 2010, the U.S. federal tax system collected about 90 percent of its revenue from taxes assessed on various types of income. Of that amount, 41 percentage points came from the personal income tax, another 40 percentage points from Social Security and Medicare taxes, and 9 percentage points from the corporate income tax. The remainder of the federal government's revenue that year (the 10 percent of total

Figure 2.5
SOCIAL SECURITY AND MEDICARE TAX RATES, 1937–2010

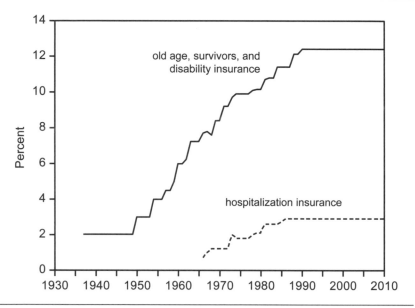

SOURCE: www.ssa.gov/OACT/ProgData/taxRates.html.

revenue that did not come from taxing income) was primarily from taxes on gifts, estates, excise taxes, and customs duties. Therefore, at the federal level, by far the most important item being taxed is income. Since wage income is the major component of household income, work is the predominant economic activity being taxed.

Most of the revenue from federal taxes on income is collected from a fairly small group of taxpayers. In the case of the personal income tax, the reason is because the first several thousand dollars of income are exempted (in 2010, the amount was $18,700 for a married couple with no dependent children), and after that amount is reached, tax rates increase along with income. Even though current top marginal tax rates are considerably lower than they were in the early 1960s, high-income families pay a disproportionate share of personal income taxes. For example, in 2008, the top 1 percent of U.S. income earners (who earned 20 percent of all income) paid 38 percent of the federal personal income tax, whereas the top 5 percent (who earned 38 percent of all income) paid 58 percent of the total.[19] For the Social Security and Medicare taxes, the effect is less pronounced because they tax labor income at a constant rate, and the Social Security tax has the income ceiling beyond which earners pay no more taxes that year. Yet it is still true that higher-income earners pay most of the taxes. In 1997, the top 30 percent of wage earners paid an estimated 58.7 percent of all Social Security taxes (Wilson 2000, charts 1 and 2).[20]

Tax systems structured this way can result in a tyranny of the majority, where the majority of voters impose their will on the minority. To see how that situation can occur, consider a simple case of a country with 100 voters who earn varying amounts of income. This country's income tax law exempts enough income so that only the top 25 income earners pay income taxes (or pay a disproportionate share of taxes). Thus, the voting population consists of 75 voters who pay no taxes or who pay only small amounts and 25 high-income workers who pay nearly all of the taxes. Now suppose this country's government is running a budget deficit (perhaps because of burdensome transfer payments to retirees) that causes political leaders to consider higher tax rates as a way to raise additional revenue. A likely outcome is that the 75 voters who are paying small amounts of taxes will support higher tax rates on the 25 who are already paying. The minority (the high-income earners) will oppose this arrangement, but they don't have the votes to block it. Of course, the situation in the United States is considerably more complicated than this simple example, but the gist of the argument is correct. It helps explain why tax increases are often directed at taxpayers who are a minority of the population. This argument applies to both high-income earners and cigarette smokers, regardless of the rationale offered by their proponents.

Defending the Transfer Payments Status Quo

The U.S. transfer payment expansion took place with widespread public support, and it was funded with income taxes. Social Security and Medicare have been popular programs, in part because many Americans appreciate having a federal "safety net" of pension income and health care insurance during their retirement years.[21] Another reason for their popularity is that many beneficiaries collect more during retirement than they paid in taxes while they were working.

Table 2.3 contains calculations on benefits and taxes paid for the Social Security OASDI and Medicare under different income scenarios. These numbers are taken from Steuerle and Rennane (2011) and assume that the income earners paid Social Security and Medicare taxes and that those funds were kept in an account that earned an inflation-adjusted interest rate of 2 percent. The calculated benefit amounts are the funds necessary upon retirement (while still earning 2 percent interest) to pay

Table 2.3

LIFETIME SOCIAL SECURITY (OASDI) AND MEDICARE (HI) TAXES AND BENEFITS FOR THOSE RETIRING AT AGE 65 IN 2010

Case 1: Single Man Earning the Average Wage ($43,100 in 2010)

OASDI Taxes	OASDI Benefits	HI Taxes	HI Benefits	Total Taxes	Total Benefits
$290,000	$256,000	$55,000	$161,000	$345,000	$417,000

Case 2: Single Woman Earning the Average Wage ($43,100 in 2010)

OASDI Taxes	OASDI Benefits	HI Taxes	HI Benefits	Total Taxes	Total Benefits
$290,000	$283,000	$55,000	$181,000	$345,000	$464,000

Case3: One-Earner Couple Earning the Average Wage ($43,100 in 2010)

OASDI Taxes	OASDI Benefits	HI Taxes	HI Benefits	Total Taxes	Total Benefits
$290,000	$435,000	$55,000	$343,000	$345,000	$778,000

Case 4: Two-Earner Couple, One Spouse Earning Average Wage ($43,100 in 2010), One Spouse Earning Low Wage ($19,400 in 2010)

OASDI Taxes	OASDI Benefits	HI Taxes	HI Benefits	Total Taxes	Total Benefits
$421,000	$457,000	$79,000	$343,000	$500,000	$800,000

Case 5: Two-Earner Couple, Each Earning Average Wage ($43,100 in 2010)

OASDI Taxes	OASDI Benefits	HI Taxes	HI Benefits	Total Taxes	Total Benefits
$581,000	$539,000	$109,000	$343,000	$690,000	$882,000

Case 6: Two-Earner Couple, One Earning High Wage ($68,900 in 2010), One Earning Average Wage ($43,100 in 2010)

OASDI Taxes	OASDI Benefits	HI Taxes	HI Benefits	Total Taxes	Total Benefits
$741,000	$645,000	$140,000	$343,000	$881,000	$988,000

SOURCE: Steuerle and Rennane (2011). OASDI = Social Security old age survivors and disability insurance taxes, and HI = Medicare hospitalization insurance taxes. Calculations assume that taxes earned an inflation-adjusted interest rate of 2.0 percent, and the benefit amounts are the dollars necessary, while earning a 2.0 percent inflation-adjusted interest rate, to make the necessary benefit payments over the expected lifetimes of the recipients.

the beneficiaries' Social Security and Medicare benefits during their expected retirement years. For example, Case 1 describes a single man who earned the average income each year during his working career (ages 22–64). He retired in 2010 at the age of 65 and began collecting

Social Security and Medicare. Assuming he lives the average life expectancy, he loses on Social Security ($290,000 in taxes paid versus $256,000 in benefits) but does well with Medicare ($55,000 paid in taxes versus $161,000 in benefits). The woman in Case 2 earned the same wage as the man in Case 1, which is why she pays the same amount in taxes, but she collects more benefits because of a longer life expectancy.

Obviously, these estimates do not apply to all U.S. workers because many earn below-average wages early in their working careers and much higher wages later. But the numbers do provide us with an idea of the tax and benefits situation. What is clear from Table 2.3 is that in many cases, participants lose on Social Security (the exceptions being Cases 3 and 4). Yet in all cases they win big on Medicare, often by large amounts. Furthermore, in all cases, total benefits exceed taxes paid. These numbers help explain the popularity of transfer payment programs, especially Medicare.

How can transfer payment programs pay out more in benefits than they collect in taxes? In part, the reason is because in each year there are enough high-wage workers paying taxes to fund the benefits to retirees; this has been the case especially while the baby boomers moved through their peak earning years. Also, any funding deficiencies can be covered from other revenue sources, including the personal income tax, as well as government borrowing. The problem on the horizon is that the upcoming large numbers of retiring baby boomers will raise the number of beneficiaries relative to workers, thereby causing major funding shortfalls for both Social Security and Medicare. Congressional efforts to reform these programs by raising the retirement age, reducing benefits, or both will likely meet stiff resistance from current or soon-to-be beneficiaries unless changes in the programs apply only to those who will be retiring several years ahead. The tyranny-of-the-majority argument suggests that a politically feasible outcome could be raising taxes on high-income earners, eliminating the Social Security tax income ceiling, or both.

The Income Tax Made It Possible

The personal income tax instituted in 1913 was originally designed to shift the burden from the working class to the upper class by taxing the top U.S. income earners and using those funds to make the federal government less dependent on customs duties and excise taxes on alcohol and tobacco. The income tax accomplished its goal, but it also created the major unintended consequence of allowing the creation of our modern big-government welfare state by generating a flood of revenue for vote-seeking politicians to spend. Supporters apparently did not foresee the income tax's ability to bring in this unprecedented revenue, but that is what happened when tax rates were raised in 1916, 1917, and 1918, in combination with the economic boom during World War I. The Republican majority that held power during the 1920s reversed this process by significantly lowering tax rates, but that proved to be temporary because the 1930s' Great Depression led to another round of major tax increases to help fund Franklin Roosevelt's New Deal, which erected the modern welfare state. The process continued after World War II, with another major change occurring in 1965 when Medicare was created.

One feature of political life that has been demonstrated repeatedly over the last several decades is the ability of politicians to spend whatever revenue is at their disposal. Over time, the U.S. economy grows, which causes tax revenue to rise. Plenty of funds are available for politicians to spend and, as we have seen, much of this increased spending has been on transfer payments. But expansions eventually end, and as the economy experiences a recession, falling incomes cause tax revenue to decline. The government budget moves into deficit (or the existing deficit expands), which causes the politicians to claim that higher tax rates are necessary to raise revenue and eliminate the deficit. This argument often carries the day because politicians and the public do not want to endure major spending cuts. Thus, tax rates are increased. This increase sets the stage for another surge in revenue when the economy expands once again.[22] Those funds get spent, and so the process continues. Stephen Moore and Richard Vedder (2010) estimate that during the period from the end of World War II to 2009, "each dollar of new tax revenue was associated with $1.17 of new spending. Politicians spend the money as fast as it comes in—and a little bit more." This process has been going on for decades, not just at the federal level but at the state and local levels as well. The federal government has spent so much that its budget deficits have been almost continuous since the early 1970s.

Here's a question to consider: when was the last time Congress significantly reduced tax rates while the federal government was running a budget surplus? In other words, when was the last time the federal government reduced tax rates so as to return a budget surplus to the taxpayers? Answer: the late 1940s.[23]

In conclusion, the historical evidence that has clearly demonstrated government's ability to grow, and at the federal level much of that growth has occurred in transfer payments. The income tax has allowed this growth to take place. Collecting taxes from one group and then handing out the benefits to another has been politically expedient because it buys votes from the beneficiaries. It has been politically feasible, in part, because those paying most of the taxes are a minority who cannot garner the votes to stop it. The process shows no sign of ending.

3. Cigarettes: Creating Crime through Taxes

With a population of 2.1 million, Cincinnati, Ohio, and its surrounding communities constitute the major metropolis in southern Ohio and northern Kentucky. The area straddles the Ohio River, and five toll-free auto bridges over that waterway allow considerable commerce between the two states. Many area residents live in one state and work in the other.

An especially brisk retail trade has long existed between Ohio and Kentucky in cigarettes and alcoholic beverages. Driving south across the river from downtown Cincinnati to Covington, Kentucky, one is struck by the abundance of tobacco and liquor stores. Over 15 such outlets are within three city blocks of the river, and the majority of their customers are from Ohio, many of whom buy several cartons of cigarettes at once. In contrast, on the Ohio side, the nearest volume tobacco and liquor stores are located about a mile from the river.[1]

Taxes explain the difference. The two states impose different levies on alcohol and, especially, cigarettes. In 2011, Ohio assessed an excise tax of $1.25 per pack of cigarettes, whereas Kentucky's rate was $0.60 per pack.[2] In other words, a carton (10 packs) of cigarettes costs $6.50 less in Kentucky than in Ohio. This large tax differential has existed for years, and based on interviews conducted in 1991, Richard Vedder reports that "42.9 percent of the cigarettes purchased by Ohioans living in the Cincinnati area . . . were bought in Kentucky" (1997, 280). The price differentials for alcoholic beverages are smaller—wine and distilled liquor cost about 10 percent less in Kentucky, whereas beer prices are roughly the same.

The two states maintain dissimilar tax rates on these products because different interest groups are at work. Kentucky is a major producer of tobacco and whiskey, whereas Ohio is not.[3] Thus, Kentucky assesses low taxes on tobacco and distilled liquor because it promotes the interests of its in-state producers. Ohio's state government is much more concerned with collecting revenue from tobacco and distilled beverage sales, and it tries to discourage tobacco consumption for public health reasons. As a result, Ohio assesses higher tax rates on those products. During fiscal year 2011, Ohio collected $794.0 million in cigarette tax revenue ($68.69 per resident), whereas Kentucky collected $262.2 million ($60.28 per resident).[4]

Officials in both states are well aware that these tax-rate differentials create an incentive for Ohioans to cross into Kentucky to purchase tobacco and liquor. Kentucky enjoys this arrangement because it collects tax revenue from residents of Ohio and other bordering states, while creating jobs in the state's retail industry. Meanwhile, Ohio's government officials realize their state is losing tax revenue to Kentucky, but they also know that their high tobacco and alcohol taxes generate more revenue than would be the case if the rates were lower.[5]

These tax rate differentials have other, more pernicious effects. Tax-created price differentials between the two states, especially for cigarettes, present smugglers with a major profit opportunity. Criminals can buy cigarettes by the truckload in Kentucky, attach counterfeit Ohio tax stamps to the bottom of each pack, and then smuggle them into Ohio where they are sold for considerably more. Cigarettes are an ideal item for this sort of activity because they are small, light, and durable. The financial returns can be enormous: in 2011, a truckload of 48,000 cartons of cigarettes would have sold for approximately $312,000 more in Ohio than they cost in Kentucky.[6]

Cigarette smuggling between Kentucky and Ohio is just the tip of the iceberg with regard to what is taking place nationally. Tobacco-producing states such as Virginia, North Carolina, and South Carolina also maintain low cigarette taxes (in 2011, Virginia charged just $0.30 per pack), while several nonproducing states tax them heavily. In 2011, Rhode Island's tax was $3.46 per pack, New York charged $4.35, and New Jersey assessed $2.70 per pack. New York City has long imposed its own levy in addition to the state tax.[7] In 2009, the city assessed $1.50 per pack, which raised the total per-pack tax (state and local) to $5.85. Imagine the profits to be made by purchasing cigarettes in Virginia ($0.30 state tax) and selling them in New York City ($5.85 combined state and city tax). High tax rates make cigarettes so valuable in New York City that shipments are routinely escorted by armed guards. In fact, throughout the United States, taxes have helped raise the retail value of cigarettes so high that stores no longer display them on the shelves with other items, but instead keep them behind the counter or under lock and key, which puts store clerks at greater risk of bodily harm by bandits.

U.S. government officials estimate that criminal organizations reap billions of dollars per year smuggling cigarettes.[8] High cigarette taxes have helped discourage smoking, but they have also led to increased crime and violence. The lure of these high profits has also created the unintended consequence of funding terrorism. There are several documented cases of terrorist organizations smuggling cigarettes to provide funding for their activities (Billingslea 2004). In many ways, the situation is remarkably similar to the case of booze during the Prohibition era, although with cigarettes the government has combined the taxes with a major education program about the hazards of smoking to help reduce demand. The situation with cigarette smuggling also demonstrates that the government doesn't necessarily need to ban a substance in order to create a crime wave. Taxes can accomplish the same outcome.

Why Cigarettes?

Taxes designed to raise revenue are most effective when they are levied on activities that do not significantly diminish when the price rises. A prime example is taxes on workers' wages. Social Security, Medicare, and income taxes all combine to significantly raise the cost of working by reducing the after-tax return on labor. Yet Americans continue to work because they need income to fund their consumption spending. Thus, governments can impose high tax rates on wage income and receive huge amounts of revenue while doing so. Similar logic explains why taxes on gasoline, alcoholic beverages, and cigarettes yield high revenue: it's because the public continues to consume large quantities despite the higher prices from the taxes on these products.

To see the interaction of tax rates and tax revenue, consider the following example as applied to cigarettes. Suppose there is a $0.50 tax on each pack of cigarettes sold, and the total cost per pack for consumers is $4.50 (consisting of the $4.00 cost of cigarettes, plus the $0.50 tax). Suppose that 1 million packs are sold each month. Total monthly spending on cigarettes is $4.5 million, of which $4 million is revenue to the sellers and $500,000 is tax revenue to the government.

Now suppose the tax is doubled to $1.00 per pack, which raises the price consumers pay to $5.00 per pack.[9] The price of cigarettes has risen by 11 percent, which will cause cigarette consumption to fall. But by how much?

Consider three scenarios:

> *1. Consumption falls by only 5 percent because cigarette consumption is unresponsive to higher prices* (because tobacco consumers are addicted to nicotine). The 5 percent decline in consumption means that sales fall from 1 million packs to 950,000 packs. Total spending on cigarettes is now $4.75 million (950,000 packs

× $5.00 per pack), of which $3.8 million is revenue to sellers (950,000 packs × $4.00 per pack) and $950,000 is tax revenue (950,000 packs × $1.00 per pack). Tax revenue has risen from $500,000 to $950,000.

2. *Consumption falls by 30 percent.* Cigarette sales decline to 700,000 packs, and $3.5 million is now being spent, with $2.8 million going to retailers and $700,000 to the government in taxes. Despite the 30 percent decline in cigarette consumption, tax revenue rises by $200,000.

3. *Cigarette consumption declines 60 percent because consumer demand is very responsive to price.* This scenario is highly improbable in the case of cigarettes, but it illustrates why governments typically do not tax products with responsive demand. Here consumption plummets to 400,000 packs. Consumers are spending $2 million on cigarettes, of which $1.6 million is revenue to sellers and $400,000 is tax revenue. The government is receiving $100,000 *less* tax revenue.

These results are summarized in Table 3.1. The reality is that cigarette tax increases produce outcomes similar to Scenario 1 because estimates of the price responsiveness of cigarette consumption suggest that a permanent 10 percent increase in price causes consumption to decline by about 4 percent in the short run, and 7.5 percent in the long run.[10] Thus, governments can raise revenue by increasing cigarette taxes. Furthermore, these tax increases are fairly easy to implement politically because most adults are nonsmokers, which means the tax is imposed on a minority of voters. Proponents of cigarette tax increases also argue that discouraging tobacco consumption benefits public health and lowers medical costs.[11]

A Golden Goose

The U.S. federal government discovered the revenue-raising abilities of tobacco taxes during the Civil War, when a tobacco tax was imposed as part of a package of excise taxes.[12] Tobacco consumption was a well-entrenched habit by this time. The primary method of consumption was chewing, but it was also taken as snuff and smoked in pipes, cigars, and cigarettes. Tobacco was part of the soldiers' rations in both the Union and Confederate armies, which stimulated its use, in part because the soldiers had a great deal of idle time on their hands (this was also the case during World Wars I and II). The 1862 law imposed a tax of 5 cents per pound on tobacco manufacturers, and taxes were levied on cigars, and then later on cigarettes. These taxes quickly proved to be a large

Table 3.1
CIGARETTE TAXES AND TAX REVENUE, ALTERNATIVE SCENARIOS

Initial situation

Price w/out Tax (per pack)	Tax (per pack)	Price incl. Tax (per pack)	Cigarette Sales (no. of packs)	Revenue	Sellers	Government
					Accruing to:	
$4.00	$0.50	$4.50	1,000,000	$4,500,000	$4,000,000	$500,000

Tax raised to $1.00 per pack[a]

Scenario 1: Sales fall 5%

Price w/out Tax (per pack)	Tax (per pack)	Price incl. Tax (per pack)	Cigarette Sales (no. of packs)	Revenue	Sellers	Government
					Accruing to:	
$4.00	$1.00	$5.00	950,000	$4,750,000	$3,800,000	$950,000

Scenario 2: Sales fall 30%

Price w/out Tax (per pack)	Tax (per pack)	Price incl. Tax (per pack)	Cigarette Sales (no. of packs)	Revenue	Sellers	Government
					Accruing to:	
$4.00	$1.00	$5.00	700,000	$3,500,000	$2,800,000	$700,000

Scenario 3: Sales fall 60%

Price w/out Tax (per pack)	Tax (per pack)	Price incl. Tax (per pack)	Cigarette Sales (no. of packs)	Revenue	Sellers	Government
					Accruing to:	
$4.00	$1.00	$5.00	400,00	$2,000,000	$1,600,000	$400,000

SOURCE: Authors calculations.
[a]Scenarios 1–3 assume that the retail price of cigarettes rises by the full amount of the tax increase.

source of revenue for the federal government: during fiscal year 1862-1863, the tobacco taxes yielded $3.1 million to the federal government, which accounted for 7.5 percent of total revenue.[13] The rates were raised again near the end of the Civil War. Afterward, as the country's population boomed and tobacco consumption became increasingly common, revenue soared. By 1875, federal revenue from tobacco taxes had risen to $37.3 million and accounted for 34 percent of total federal tax revenue.

Rise of the Cigarette

Before the 1880s, prerolled cigarettes were expensive to produce because they were hand-rolled (like cigars). A worker could roll about four cigarettes per minute, or roughly 2,400 during a 10-hour workday. This process made cigarettes expensive, and since many smokers did not want to go to the trouble of rolling their own, tobacco was smoked primarily in pipes. This situation changed in the 1880s, when James

Bonsack developed the cigarette-rolling machine. By 1884, it allowed three workers to produce 120,000 cigarettes per day (Robert 1949, 142). Cigarette prices fell, further assisted by the federal government's reduction in tobacco tax rates that same decade.

Falling prices raised cigarettes' popularity. Sales by tobacco companies soared from 9 million cigarettes in 1885 to 60 million in 1887 (Burns 2007, 135). Then, during the 1890s, the industry developed faster rolling machines and better-tasting tobaccos and was further aided by the development of safer matches. In the midst of this boom in cigarette sales, in 1898 the federal government raised excise taxes on tobacco (and several other products) to help pay for the Spanish-American War. Revenue rose substantially; from 1897 to 1899, tobacco tax revenue increased from $30.7 million to $59.3 million (U.S. Bureau of the Census 1975, 1108).

Booming cigarette sales during the 1910s caused smoking to displace chewing as the preferred method of tobacco consumption. This process was aided greatly by World War I because the U.S. Army ordered massive amounts of cigarettes for the troops serving overseas, and huge quantities were donated as well. Millions of new nicotine addicts were created, and arguments about tobacco's negative health effects did not carry much weight to soldiers concerned about surviving their ordeal in the trenches. After the war, the U.S. tobacco industry boomed along with the national economy. Cigarettes were aggressively marketed with clever ad lines ("I'd walk a mile for a Camel") and commercials on radio. Prominent Americans appeared in public with lit cigarettes in hand, and increasing numbers of women were smoking (and drinking alcohol) in public. Rising tobacco demand fueled excise tax revenues; by 1930, tobacco tax levies were generating $450 million of revenue, which was 15 percent of that year's federal tax collections (U.S. Bureau of the Census 1975, 1107).

State Taxes

During the tobacco boom of the late 1800s and early 1900s, critics argued that tobacco consumption was unhealthy and disgusting, although the critics generally preferred smoking over chewing. A prohibition effort was under way similar to the one against alcohol, and between 1895 and 1921, it led 14 states to prohibit or place limitations on cigarettes. However, by 1927, most of these laws had been either repealed or watered down, although sales to minors were still restricted in many places. The anti-tobacco crusade was not nearly as successful as the one against alcohol, partly because the clergy never became major backers. Also, although tobacco use imposes costs, they are borne largely by the users as the habit does not cause them to be impaired, lose their jobs, or beat their spouses and children.[14]

The tobacco prohibitionists did, however, provide some of the impetus for states to impose their own taxes on tobacco, although the states' primary motivation was to raise revenue to help eliminate budget deficits (Robert 1949, 256). In 1921, Iowa became the first state to impose a cigarette tax, and by 1930, when the Great Depression was beginning to ravage state budgets, a dozen states were taxing tobacco. The trend continued, and by 1941, 27 states had tobacco taxes in place. A typical state tax rate was 2 or 3 cents per pack.

Cigarette Smuggling

Interstate tobacco smuggling began in the 1920s with the imposition of state cigarette taxes, and by the late 1930s, it was flourishing in many places, especially New York City. In 1938, the city imposed a temporary 1-cent per-pack tax (a pack cost about 15 cents at the time), and the following year the state of New York enacted a 2-cent tax. Meanwhile, New Jersey did not have a cigarette tax. Thus, an ideal situation was created for smuggling: a no-tax location (New Jersey) located across a river (the Hudson) from a heavily populated high-tax area (New York City).

The original smugglers were essentially door-to-door salesmen and street vendors. The salesmen made the rounds of apartment buildings and offices, taking cigarette orders and then filling them by traveling out of state to make the purchases. One customer described the arrangement to a state commission: "Every Monday [he] came and took your order. Every Wednesday [he] delivered it . . . [he] was just as regular as a milkman" (Fleenor 2003, 6). Vendors sold smuggled cigarettes on street corners and in subway and railroad stations. During the 1940s and 1950s, these operations were relatively small-scale and unorganized because the tax rates were low, which limited the profit opportunity.[15] However, tax avoidance was a big enough problem that it led Congress to pass the 1949 Jenkins Act, which requires those who sell or transport cigarettes into a state to report the information to that state's taxing authority.

Cigarette smuggling intensified in the mid-1960s, when several states raised their tax rates. The key event occurred in January 1964, when the U.S. surgeon general issued the now-famous report linking smoking with respiratory problems, heart disease, lung cancer, and low birth weight. That report was the motivation for several states to significantly raise their cigarette taxes in an effort to discourage smoking. By the end of 1965, half the states had raised rates, in many cases by substantial amounts. For example, Colorado imposed its first cigarette tax at 3 cents per pack, Arizona's levy went from 2.0 to 6.5 cents, Hawaii's from 3.9 to 8.0 cents, Illinois's from 4 to 7 cents, and New York doubled its rate from 5 cents to 10 cents. Interestingly, Virginia *lowered* its rate from 3.0 to 2.5 cent per pack.[16]

These tax increases widened the price differential among states, and in doing so raised the profitability of cigarette smuggling by enough to attract organized crime. According to Fleenor, by the late 1960s in New York (and by extension elsewhere), the mob had taken over the smuggling business and shoved out the small operators. Among these criminals were "former alcohol bootleggers who had honed their smuggling skills during Prohibition" (Fleenor 2003, 7). And as had taken place during the 1920s, the criminal gangs used violence to control the trade. They fought territorial wars, hijacked shipments, and coerced retailers into selling their cigarettes. Organized crime has been heavily involved in the cigarette trade ever since.

New York responded by increasing the penalties for cigarette smuggling and raising enforcement efforts, but it was a losing battle. In 1970, the state seized 100,000 cartons of illegal cigarettes, this at a time when it was estimated that 110,000 cartons were smuggled into the state *daily* (Fleenor 2003, 9–10). In 1974, Governor Malcolm Wilson described New York City as the "promised land" for cigarette smugglers and proposed a plan where the city would repeal its cigarette tax in an effort to reduce crime, and the state would make up the lost revenue.[17] The federal government became involved in 1978 when the Contraband Cigarette Act became law, making it a federal crime to smuggle cigarettes across state lines to avoid state cigarette taxes. Ironically, many argued that the law had the unintended consequence of causing increased theft of in-state cigarettes (Fleenor 2003, 11).

At about this time, the smuggling problem lessened somewhat because the business became less profitable. Rising U.S. inflation in the mid-1970s caused nonindexed tax rates in effect to decline, which affected both states' budgets and smugglers' profits. States such as Michigan, which held its cigarette tax rates constant (as many states did during the 1970s), suffered a decline in inflation-adjusted revenue of roughly 40 percent from 1976 to 1981 (Michigan Department of Treasury 2005, 9). This falling inflation-adjusted revenue meant that the return to smuggling was falling as well because the inflation-adjusted tax-rate differentials among states were narrowing.[18] In addition, smugglers incurred greater shipping costs because of higher petroleum prices associated with the 1970s energy crisis.

However, this situation did not persist. States initiated another round of major tax increases in the early 1990s and by doing so brought smuggling back in a big way. States were facing budgetary problems due to the

1990–1991 recession. In addition, government payments for health care were rising, and the argument was made that some of those increased health care costs could be blamed on smoking. States began to push for cigarette tax increases, which were relatively easy to institute because smokers were not only a minority, but a shrinking one; the proportion of U.S. adults who smoked had been falling since the 1970s. Several states imposed major increases in cigarette taxes during the 1990s, and if a particular state did not raise its rates then, it most likely did during the 2000s. Table 3.2 provides cigarette tax rates for 1990 and 2011 in selected states. Not only did states raise their rates by huge amounts, the spread between high-tax states and low-tax states increased enormously.

Once again, this widening of the state tax rate differentials made interstate cigarette smuggling more profitable. By 2011, cigarettes pur-

Table 3.2
CIGARETTE TAX RATES IN SELECTED STATES, 1990 & 2011

State	Tax Rate in Effect 1/1/1990 (cents per pack)	Tax Rate in Effect 1/1/2011 (cents per pack)
Alaska	29.0	200.0
Arizona	15.0	200.0
Connecticut	40.0	340.0
Maryland	13.0	200.0
Michigan	25.0	200.0
New Jersey	27.0	270.0
New York	33.0	435.0
Ohio	18.0	125.0
Rhode Island	37.0	346.0
Texas	26.0	141.0
Vermont	17.0	262.0
Washington	34.0	302.5
***		
Kentucky	3.0	60.0
Missouri	13.0	17.0
North Carolina	2.0	45.0
South Carolina	7.0	57.0
Virginia	2.5	30.0

SOURCE: *The Tax Burden on Tobacco: Historical Compilation 2007*, pp. 9–10, and Campaign for Tobacco-Free Kids, www.tobaccofreekids.org.

chased in Virginia (with the $0.30 per-pack tax) could be illegally transported to New York City ($5.85 tax per pack) and sold for $5.55 more per pack. That adds up to $55.50 per carton, or $2.664 million per truckload of 48,000 cartons. With financial returns of this magnitude, is it any wonder why organized crime and terrorist groups are involved?

Cigarette Scams

Three companies—R. J. Reynolds, Altria, and Lorillard—account for roughly 90 percent of the cigarettes produced in the United States. Their production facilities consist of a few enormous factories located in Virginia, North Carolina, and Kentucky. When cigarettes leave those factories, they are moved to warehouses, at which point the federal excise tax (raised from $0.39 to $1.01 per pack in 2009) is paid. Since so few firms and factories account for such a large proportion of cigarette production, the federal government can monitor the situation and ensure that wholesalers are paying the tax. Some cigarettes are exempt from this tax: those designated for shipment to duty-free shops, Indian reservations in the United States, and U.S. military bases for sale at the base exchange, or those bound for export to other countries.

For cigarettes destined for the regular taxable domestic market, the next step is to pay the state taxes. These taxes are paid by a wholesaler stamping agent, which is a business that has the authority to buy tax stamps from the various states and attach them to the packs of cigarettes. Once these taxes are paid, the cigarettes are shipped off to other wholesalers or directly to retailers for sale in the state where the taxes have been paid. At each step in this process, the number of organizations and governments involved grows larger. And with billions of packs of cigarettes changing hands each year, monitoring becomes extremely difficult.

There are several opportunities to avoid cigarette taxes:

1. Perhaps the most common method is to set up a wholesaling operation that is really two operations: one legal, the other illegal. The legal portion buys cigarettes directly from manufacturers, pays the federal and state taxes, and then ships the product to where they are supposed to go. Meanwhile, a second operation purchases cigarettes from a "friendly" wholesaler located in a low-tax state and pays that wholesaler *not* to affix state tax stamps (this would be somewhat easier in North Carolina because that state does not require tax stamps). The unscrupulous wholesaler then attaches counterfeit state tax stamps and ships them in what is called "over-the-road" smuggling. A variant of

this operation is to buy legitimate state tax stamps, cut them in half so the stamps go twice as far, and then hope that the retailers and customers do not report the altered tax stamps to states' authorities.

2. A "diversion" operation involves a wholesaler buying cigarettes from manufacturers, paying the federal excise tax, but then reporting only a portion of those purchases to state agencies.[19] This operation is riskier (and therefore believed to be considerably less common) because investigators can cross-check records and identify the fraud.

3. Cross-border shopping is a major method of avoiding taxes. This method takes place both on a small scale, such as when Ohioans drive to Kentucky to purchase a few cartons for their own consumption, and on a much larger scale when the number of cigarettes purchased fills a small truck that is then driven to the high-tax jurisdiction where the cigarettes are sold. Cross-border shopping also takes place when Americans purchase cigarettes in Mexico and when military personnel buy cigarettes at a base exchange for their nonmilitary friends and families.

4. To legally produce cigarettes in the United States, a permit is required from the Alcohol and Tobacco Tax and Trade Bureau, the office responsible for collecting federal excise taxes on alcohol and tobacco. "Bootleg" manufacturing operations are firms that produce cigarettes without the required permit and then sell them through cooperating retailers.[20]

5. Cigarettes bound for export, for sale on Indian reservations, at duty-free shops, or on military bases are exempt from both federal and state taxes.[21] This exemption creates several possibilities for tax evasion. One obvious method is to purchase cigarettes from U.S. manufacturers, export them to another country, and then smuggle them back into the United States. Selling them through a "friendly" U.S. retailer would allow tax-free cigarettes to be sold at the same price as taxed cigarettes. This type of smuggling is certainly going on, not only through neighboring Mexico and Canada but through several other countries as well because cigarettes are cheap to transport. With thousands of shipping containers entering the United States each day, the likelihood of U.S. Customs agents discovering one filled with smuggled cigarettes is small, especially when investigators are more concerned about terrorist activities.

Another scheme is to work up phony paperwork showing that cigarettes are destined for military base exchanges or duty-free shops when in fact they are not. This arrangement would be somewhat difficult to carry out because records exist about how many cigarettes actually arrive on military bases and at duty-free shops. But again, with billions of packs of cigarettes being bought and sold in the United States each year, monitoring is an issue.

Indian reservations present a major opportunity to take advantage of the tax exemption. Legally, Indian reservations are independent nations, meaning they can import cigarettes tax-free. Many Native American tribes have taken advantage of the exemption by establishing retail operations selling tax-free cigarettes (and petroleum products). Consumers can purchase these cigarettes either by traveling to the reservations or by ordering online or by telephone and receiving them through the mail. Several states have attempted to stop this practice by passing laws requiring the tribes to charge taxes on cigarettes sold to buyers who are not members of the tribe, and the U.S. Supreme Court has ruled these laws constitutional. However, there are concerns that retailers on some reservations are not following this rule. Furthermore, a few states (e.g., New York) have passed such laws but have not enforced them with consistency. In fact, there have been widespread allegations in New York that some Indian retailers are selling enormous quantities of cigarettes to smugglers who transport them off the reservations where they are sold at significantly higher prices.

A Big Business

No one knows precisely how many cigarettes are being shipped and sold each year in the United States to avoid taxes, but the number is huge. In the words of Paul Carey III of the Northern Virginia Cigarette Tax Board, "It's a big business and it's getting horribly bigger."[22] Consider that from 1995 to 2007 the proportion of U.S. adults who reported being smokers fell from 22.7 percent to 19.8 percent (a 2.9 percentage point drop), while adult per capita sales of cigarettes *subject to state taxes* fell from 121 packs to 78.4 packs (a 35 percent decline).[23]

Several studies attempt to estimate the quantity of contraband cigarette sales, and they begin by noting the enormous variation in state-taxed per capita sales. For example, here are the states with the highest and lowest values for 2007:

State	Per Capita Taxed Sales (no. of packs)
Delaware	185.2
Kentucky	141.9
Washington	32.4
New York	32.3
Median state	58.6

Source: Orzechowski and Walker (2007, 40).

These orders of magnitude are much greater than can be explained by varying population demographics, income, and cigarette prices among the states listed. In fact, what these data tell us is that unequal cigarette tax rates among states cause considerable smuggling and cross-border shopping. Also, the existence of military bases and Indian reservations in certain states (e.g., New York and Washington) help explain their low taxed sales.

Delaware had exceptionally high sales because of lower cigarette taxes than neighboring states. On January 1, 2007, Delaware's tax was $0.55 per pack, whereas the tax in Pennsylvania was $1.35, New Jersey charged $2.57, and Maryland's levy was $1.00. There was considerable incentive to cross-border shop, made easy by Delaware's proximity to metropolitan Philadelphia. Meanwhile, New York's high taxes provided incentive for that state's smokers to buy from low-tax sources, and for smugglers to bring cigarettes in from outside the state or from the Indian reservations.[24]

Generally speaking, studies of the magnitude of the U.S. contraband cigarette trade suggest that the amounts have varied considerably over time, largely because of changing state tax-rate differentials and enforcement efforts by government.[25] Jerry and Marie Thursby estimate that from 1972 to 1990, the amount of U.S. commercial smuggling (including cross-border shopping) ranged from a low of less than 1 percent of total sales to a high of over 7 percent (Thursby and Thursby 2000). Since 1990, smuggling is believed to have become much more prevalent because of rising state tax-rate differentials. Patrick Fleenor (1998) considers taxable sales lost to cross-border shopping, smuggling, and sales on military bases and Indian reservations from the early 1960s to the late 1990s. His results suggest that in 1962, a few years before the big state tax increases took place, 5.6 percent of cigarette sales were made through cross-border activity. The state-tax increases that took place during the 1960s raised the number to 11.1 percent by 1972, but then falling inflation-adjusted tax rates combined with tougher laws against smuggling drove it down to 5.4 percent by 1982. Since that time, contraband sales have gone up, almost certainly by a large amount. The state tax increases that took place during the 1980s and 1990s made smuggling more profitable, and Fleenor's estimates suggest that by 1997, 13.3 percent of all cigarettes sold in the United States were avoiding taxes, of which more than half of that amount (7.8 percent) was smuggled. The remainder was in cross-border sales and transactions on military bases and Indian reservations.[26] More recently, the U.S. Bureau of Alcohol, Tobacco, and Firearms estimates that states are losing about $5 billion in tax revenue per year because of smuggling. During fiscal year 2008, states collected about $20 billion in cigarette taxes (both excise and sales tax), so a rough estimate would suggest that about 20 percent of cigarettes consumed per year in the United States are being smuggled or are being bought and sold in a manner to avoid taxes.[27]

Cigarette Empires in the Empire State

The Poospatuck Reservation on New York's Long Island is one of the state's cigarette-retailing powerhouses. Consisting of roughly one square mile of land and about 270 residents, the reservation imported over 100 million packs of cigarettes during 2007. Those cigarettes were then resold through retail outlets and Internet sales.[28] An even larger quantity—125 million packs—were handled on the Seneca tribe's two reservations in western New York. These cigarettes were sold to consumers not just in New York but throughout the country. Lost revenue to New York's state and local governments is estimated to be nearly $1 billion per year.[29]

The existence of several Indian reservations in New York goes a long way toward explaining that state's exceptionally low per capita taxed cigarette sales. In fact, during the last several years, an interesting battle over taxes has taken place there between the state government and the Indian tribes. Not only have the tribes established retail outlets on their reservations where consumers can buy tax-free tobacco and petroleum products, they also set up operations that accept cigarette orders over the Internet and by phone, and ship through the mail. In addition, authorities believe that huge amounts of cigarettes are being sold to smugglers, who ship them off the reservations to retailers within the state.

In fact, Indian reservation sales are huge: during 2007 (which was *before* New York raised its cigarette tax from $1.50 to $2.75 per pack), about 304 million packs of cigarettes were sold by retailers on the state's Indian reservations.[30] That same year, New York collected taxes on 622 million packs.[31]

Not surprisingly, Indian reservation sales have been a hot topic for years in New York (and in other states with Indian reservations). Convenience store operators have been among the most vocal critics because they lose cigarette sales to the tribes. New York's state legislature attempted to force the Indians to collect cigarette taxes by passing a law specifying that reservation sales could be tax-free only to tribe members, but the tribes ignored it, claiming that they are not subject to the law because they are independent nations. The Seneca have been particularly aggressive on this point because they have an 1842 treaty with the

United States government that "protect[s] the Seneca from all taxes."[32] In April 1997, the New York State Police imposed an embargo against the Seneca to prevent tobacco and petroleum products from entering their reservations. A large group of Seneca and their supporters organized a mass protest that turned violent, resulting in several injuries and arrests, and the shutdown of two major freeways passing through the reservations when protestors set fire to tires blocking the roads.[33] Since then, the state has attempted to force the wholesalers (who supply the Indians) to collect the tax, but a court injunction has prevented that from happening. The state has tried repeatedly to persuade the Indians to collect the taxes on purchases by non-Indians, but the tribes have not only continued to refuse, they have threatened further actions. Among other ideas, the Seneca have discussed placing toll booths on Interstate 90 to collect fees from every vehicle passing through the reservation. Tribal leaders have also authorized the tribe's president to ask the president of the United States for federal troops to protect the reservation against actions by New York State.[34]

Funding Terrorism

Government officials in the United States and elsewhere believe that international terrorist organizations became involved in large-scale cigarette smuggling during the 1990s. That activity stemmed from the large cigarette tax increases of the late 1980s and early 1990s that took place in the United States, the United Kingdom, and Europe (Billingslea 2004). Here again, no one knows the scale of that smuggling activity, but it is believed to be large and extremely profitable.

Examples abound. The terrorists who exploded the bomb beneath New York's World Trade Center in 1993 had counterfeit cigarette stamps in their apartment (Fleenor 2008). The Irish Republican Army is estimated to have earned $100 million over a five-year period starting in the late 1990s by smuggling cigarettes and hijacking shipping containers (Billingslea 2004). Before his downfall, Saddam Hussein was smuggling cigarettes into Iraq from Turkey in violation of the economic sanctions in place at the time, allegedly earning billions of dollars while doing so. Hussein's son Uday—who achieved infamy for murdering a man at a banquet attended by the first lady of Egypt and having members of the Iraqi national soccer team tortured after losing matches—was in charge of the cigarette smuggling operation.[35] In the United States, a ring of smugglers was arrested in 2000 and later convicted for smuggling $7.9 million worth of cigarettes from low-tax North Carolina to high-tax Michigan. Their profits, estimated at $1.5 million, were channeled to Hezbollah.[36] Although $1.5 million is not a huge sum of money, consider that the September 11, 2001, attacks are estimated to have cost the terrorists $300,000 to $500,000 (U.S. General Accounting Office 2003, 6). In 2005, a Buffalo, New York, businessman was caught smuggling cigarettes. Federal investigators said he was using the funds to support "scholarships" at terrorist training camps in Afghanistan (Fleenor 2008).

These are some of the cases that law enforcement authorities know about. There are likely many more that are as yet unknown. Given the number of cigarettes being produced and consumed around the world each year and the high tax rates imposed by many jurisdictions, the potential for mischief is enormous. And authorities cannot begin to track them all; to cite just one example of freight volume, the Los Angeles–Long Beach harbor, which is believed to be a major port for imported contraband cigarettes, handles about 9,000 shipping containers daily. With several major ports around the world, there is simply no way to effectively monitor that amount of cargo.

Prohibition Redux?

With alcohol Prohibition during the 1920s, the United States managed to create a major crime problem by banning the product. In the case of cigarettes, a similar outcome, although on a smaller scale, has been created through taxes. One can only imagine the crime wave that would hit the United States if authorities ever attempted to ban tobacco.

As long as governments treat cigarettes as a plum to be picked for tax revenue, the problem will continue. And just as occurred during Prohibition, we can expect it to grow over time as criminal organizations perfect their business model, battle over territories, and expand their activities. As governments tax cigarettes ever more heavily—almost a certainty as state and local governments experience budgetary problems brought on by the 2007–2009 economic recession and the slow-growth economy that followed it—the crime problem will get worse. There will be no way to stop it unless the public—through its elected representatives—decides to significantly increase the resources devoted to enforcement, makes penalties more severe, and is willing to imprison large numbers of Americans for evading cigarette taxes.

At one point during the 1990s, the Canadians had raised cigarette taxes to such heights that it caused a huge amount of smuggling. Major increases in cigarette taxes at both the federal and provincial level from 1984 to 1993 raised the inflation-adjusted price of a pack of cigarettes (in 1994 dollars) from $2.64 to $5.65 in parts of Canada. The purpose of those increases was to raise revenue and discourage smoking. However, those enormous tax increases set off a wave of smuggling, largely in the form of cigarettes that were exported tax-free from Canada to the United States and then brought back into the country illegally. Cigarette imports from Canada to the United States increased 11-fold from 1990 to 1993, with many of them passing through the St. Regis Mohawk Indian Reservation in New York, which straddles the U.S.-Canadian border. Profits were estimated to be $500,000 Canadian per truckload. In Quebec, an estimated 60 percent of all cigarettes were contraband.[37]

Canadians recognized the magnitude of the smuggling problem and the flourishing black market for cigarettes. Among the many problems it created, minors were finding it easy to buy cigarettes in the illegal market, which was certainly not a desired result of high cigarette taxes. The Canadian federal and provincial governments concluded that high tax rates had been a failure and rolled them back, by $2.10 per pack in Quebec and $1.92 in Ontario. By 1996, U.S. cigarette imports from Canada had dropped by 96 percent.

4. The Minimum Wage: Promoting Teenage Unemployment

> *It is breathtakingly stupid to think of minimum wages as an anti-poverty tool. If it were, poverty in Haiti, Ethiopia and Bangladesh could be instantly eliminated simply by proposing that their legislators mandate a higher minimum wage.*

—Walter Williams (2010a)

Here's a sure-fire way to make us rich: have the government pass a law stating that, effective tomorrow, no jobholder in the United States shall be paid less than $1,000 per hour. Regardless of the type of work—truck driver, brain surgeon, janitor, attorney, schoolteacher—every jobholder will earn at least $1,000 for every hour worked. That works out (before taxes) to $8,000 per eight-hour day, $40,000 per week, $2.08 million per year. Our standard of living would soar to unprecedented heights and poverty would be wiped out, all thanks to a simple wage regulation imposed by the government.

Unfortunately, that's not how it would turn out. If the government imposed a minimum wage of that magnitude, the result would be massive unemployment. The only workers who would keep their jobs would be those creating at least $1,000 of value for an hour's work, and that describes only a tiny fraction of the workforce. Top professional athletes and entertainers would still be employed, at least as long as the rest of us were willing to pay to watch them perform. Some business executives would keep their jobs, although many companies would collapse into bankruptcy. Most everyone else would be laid off. After all, if you were an employer who had to pay every worker at least $1,000 per hour, which employees would you retain? Some businesses might continue to employ their workers and pass on the higher labor costs by charging much higher prices for their products, but price increases of the magnitude necessary to cover such an enormous increase in costs would cause sales to plummet. Companies would soon discover that they'd be better off closing down their operations and laying off the workers. In the end, a law designed to make everyone rich would, in fact, have the unintended consequence of making most of us poor instead.

Of course, the federal minimum wage is not $1,000 per hour, but instead $7.25 per hour.[1] At this level, the minimum wage does not cause major unemployment and poverty, but it does help create those problems on a small scale. Most affected are teenagers and high school dropouts because they often lack the skills necessary to create $7.25 of value while working for an hour. They might be willing to work for less than the minimum, but employers are reluctant to hire under those conditions because doing so would violate the law. Some low-skilled workers can find jobs at the minimum wage, so the law benefits them because they earn more than they would if the law did not exist. In this way, a minimum wage creates winners and losers: the winners are those earning a higher wage because of the law; the losers are those who earn nothing because they have been priced out of jobs.

Minimum wage laws were originally designed to accomplish the honorable goal of raising incomes of the working poor. However, their success in achieving that outcome is in serious doubt. In fact, the minimum wage law is another example of a well-intentioned law with adverse unintended consequences. Artificially raising wages elevates the incomes of *some* low-skilled workers—those employed at or slightly above the minimum—but lowers the incomes of those unable to find work, many of whom might be willing to work for less than the minimum. In addition, artificially raising the wage rate creates a surplus of unskilled workers, which enhances the ability of employers to discriminate. Furthermore, by preventing many teenagers from working, the law denies them the opportunity to gain valuable experience, which would help make them more productive later in life.

A Living Wage

Christian theologians have long argued that a worker has a natural right to earn an income that supports a basic standard of living. In the 13th century, Thomas Aquinas said that commodities (agricultural products) should fetch a fair price, and workers should earn a just wage. Those willing and able to work should earn an income sufficient to provide their families with the basic necessities of life.[2]

Harsh realities of the marketplace, however, have long conflicted with this lofty ideal. During the Middle Ages, peasant farmers lived a subsistence life, consuming most of what they produced (after paying a share to the landowning noble). A large segment of the population was malnourished and susceptible to disease, which is why droughts or other adverse growing conditions were so devastating. Reductions in food output caused serious hunger and, if the situation was bad enough, starvation. The bubonic plague, which wiped out an estimated one-third to one-half of Europe's population during the mid-1300s, came on the heels of several consecutive years of poor harvests that had left the population severely weakened and ripe for destruction. In a world like that, how was a worker going to earn a "just wage?"

The living wage concept moved to the forefront during the Industrial Revolution. Industrialization raised living standards generally, but especially for some capitalists who became extremely wealthy. As a result, a major widening of the gap occurred between the rich and the working class. Imagine being a steelworker in 1890s' Homestead, Pennsylvania, earning $2 for a 12-hour workday spent doing extremely dangerous tasks in searing heat near an open blast furnace, and then going home to a squalid tenement in the shadows of the belching mill. Meanwhile, the owner of the steel company, Andrew Carnegie, earned millions of dollars each year and lived a life of incredible luxury. Such conditions made the "living wage" appealing to the working class, *and attainable because the rich capitalists could afford to pay it.*

During this era, social reformers advocated for a living wage, in addition to pushing for the end of several labor practices they considered offensive. One major issue of the day was child labor; many Americans were appalled by the number of children from low-income families working in factories, canneries, meatpacking plants, textile mills, and mines and on farms. By 1900, over a million U.S. children were employed at such locations, often enduring horrid conditions while being paid much lower wages than adults. For example, youths earned $0.25 for a 12- to 14-hour day working in coal mines, and $1.50–$2.50 per week toiling in factories (Bettmann 1974, 77–79). At that time, adult laborers earned about $2 for a 12-hour day. Social reformers believed that children would be better off in school than working, and that would be more likely to happen if their parents earned a living wage. Another argument against child labor was that since children were willing to work for lower wages than adults, they displaced adult men in the workforce. Therefore, the logic ran, if the government raised wage rates, children would be priced out of jobs and employers would hire adults instead. This view is a major reason why organized labor backed the minimum wage. The unions saw it as a way to induce employers to replace non-union workers (which included women and children) with adult male union workers.

Another major issue was the plight of working women. The prevailing view at the time was that women would work until they married, at which time they would quit their jobs and their husbands would support them. Women who worked were usually employed as domestic help or in factories, and social reformers argued that those women also deserved a living wage. Since women were willing to work for lower wages than men (especially for factory work), a wage floor would provide working women with a living wage, and also cause some of them to lose their jobs and be replaced by men.[3] Reformers also pointed out that women employed in manufacturing establishments often endured atrocious working conditions. The 1911 Triangle Shirtwaist factory fire in New York City that killed over 140 women employed in a sweatshop did much to raise public support for improved working conditions.

Based on these arguments, Massachusetts passed the nation's first minimum wage law in 1912. It created a Minimum Wage Commission that was given authority to set minimum wage rates in various industries. These wages applied to women and children, and were based on estimates of both the cost of living and employers' ability to pay.[4] Other states soon followed, and by 1923, 17 states had enacted minimum wage legislation. In many cases, these laws were similar to Massachusetts in that their minimum wages applied only to women and children. That same year, however, the movement received a serious blow when the U.S. Supreme Court declared Washington, D.C.'s law unconstitutional on the grounds that it violated the principle of freedom of contract (U.S Department of Labor 1967, 9–11). During the next two years, this decision was used as the basis to declare five states' minimum wage statutes unconstitutional and led several other states to repeal their laws. The movement was further hindered by the major U.S. economic boom taking place during the 1920s. Rising demand for workers and tightened immigration caused market-determined wages to rise and working conditions to improve. It was no longer clear to many Americans that government intervention was needed to raise workers' incomes.

The Great Depression

The economic boom ended in 1929 when the United States plunged into the Great Depression (1929–1941). A series of monumental economic policy errors committed during the late 1920s and early 1930s caused economic activity in the United States and elsewhere to fall precipitously. The labor force unemployment rate, which was 3.2 percent in the final boom year of 1929, soared to 25.2 percent in 1933, when an estimated 13 million U.S. workers were unemployed.[5] In fact, conditions were even worse than the official statistics indicate because many of those fortunate enough to still have jobs suffered severe reductions in the number of hours worked per week.

The drastic worsening of economic conditions during the early 1930s brought new life to the minimum wage movement. The huge employment declines were accompanied by falling wages, and many viewed these wage cuts as a major cause of workers' falling incomes. Although it is true that those *with jobs* who experienced wage cuts ended up earning less, it is also true that even more jobs would have been lost if wages had not fallen. Millions of workers had lost their jobs because, in part, their wages were too high. In other words, plummeting spending on goods and services had reduced the number of workers that businesses were willing to employ, and a policy of propping up labor costs by preventing wages from falling would result in even more unemployment. Yet most people did not view the situation that way. Instead, they ignored the disemployment effect of higher wages and argued that a government-imposed minimum wage would support workers' incomes. President Herbert Hoover accepted the falling-wages-are-the-problem explanation, and in the early 1930s, while the economy was plunging into an ever-deeper hole, he urged the business community to maintain wage rates. Incoming President Franklin Roosevelt also supported this view and believed that workers deserved a "fair" wage.

So the abysmal labor market conditions during the Great Depression altered public opinion, and by doing so set the stage for the nation's first federal minimum wage law. A sizable segment of the public and political leaders joined organized labor and social reformers in supporting wage regulation. The minimum wage was included as part of the New Deal's 1933 National Industrial Recovery Act (NIRA). The NIRA was a comprehensive program of industry and labor regulation based on the flawed notion that encouraging businesses to band together and cooperate (instead of competing against each other) would help promote economic recovery. The NIRA instructed industries to write up codes of "fair competition," which were agreements designed to control the behavior of the firms in each industry. The codes included anti-competitive devices, such as setting minimum prices, standardizing products, regulating hours of operation, and preventing companies from defaming their competitors.[6] That firms would conspire to behave anti-competitively when given permission by the government is predictable because, as the great economist Adam Smith so famously pointed out in *The Wealth of Nations*, "People of the same trade seldom meet together, even for merriment and diversion, but the conversation ends in a conspiracy against the public, or in some contrivance to raise prices" (Smith [1776] 1993, 144). What is amazing is that businesses were being urged by the government to meet and conspire and were exempted from U.S. antitrust laws while doing so.

The minimum wage was included in the codes' labor provisions. Industries were allowed to set their own minimum wage, but the so-called blanket code (imposed by the Roosevelt administration in the summer of 1933) included a minimum wage of $0.25 per hour, which was scheduled to rise to $0.40 seven years later. The blanket code also included many of the social reformers' goals, such as a shorter work-week (44 hours) and prohibitions on child labor.[7] Several industries' codes specified higher minimum wages; the average across all industries was $0.30 per hour (Paulsen 1996, 47).

Minimum wage supporters were disappointed with this initial federal attempt at wage regulation. One major complaint was with the wage itself: $0.25 per hour earned over a 44-hour week translated into an annual income of $550 ($11/week × 50 workweeks/year). This amount was below everyone's estimate of a "living wage" for a northern U.S. city. Supporters were also upset because some key industries, such as farming and household help, were exempted. Another source of disappointment was the fact that the NIRA did not appear to promote recovery. Although the economy improved somewhat in 1933, labor market conditions remained weak. The unemployment rate, which peaked at 25.2 percent in 1933, was 20.3 percent in 1935. Some believed that the minimum wage rules were partly responsible for the continuing high unemployment. Meanwhile, there were claims that the minimum wage law had not benefited U.S. workers as a group because businesses had raised the wages of unskilled workers while reducing the wages of skilled workers.

Thus, by the mid-1930s, the public had concluded that the NIRA had failed to promote economic recovery. This outcome is not surprising when we consider that the thrust of the law was to raise business costs and reduce competition among firms. In fact, the NIRA was so unpopular that many Americans were delighted when in 1935 the U.S. Supreme Court declared the NIRA unconstitutional.[8] Yet despite the failure of the NIRA, the public continued to support regulation of wages and working conditions; those provisions of the NIRA were resurrected a few years later in the 1938 Fair Labor Standards Act. The minimum wage was once again set at $0.25 per hour and was scheduled to rise to $0.30 in 1939, and then to $0.40 in 1945. The United States has had a federal minimum wage ever since.

The Early Years

Economists believe that the minimum wage rates imposed by the 1938 Fair Labor Standards Act did not have a major impact on U.S. labor market conditions during the first several years they were in place. One reason is that they were below the prevailing wage for unskilled workers in many areas of the United States. Also, in places where the minimum wage was binding, the law was often ignored. Furthermore, during the early 1940s, the U.S. employment situation improved considerably when the nation began to militarize in response to events in Europe and Asia and then became a full-fledged combatant at the end of 1941. The U.S. unemployment rate fell rapidly as a result:

Year	Unemployment Rate
1938	19.1 %
1939	17.2 %
1940	14.6 %
1941	9.9 %
1942	4.7 %
1943	1.9 %

Source: R. J. Gordon (2000, app. A).

The minimum wage rates did not hinder employment growth in any meaningful way, and this was true after World War II as well. Table 4.1 contains data on employment and wages from 1938 to 1950, and you can see that both measures rose significantly as the U.S. economy recovered from the Great Depression and then mobilized for World War II. The minimum wage fell as a percentage of the average wage paid in manufacturing, bottoming out in 1944 at 29 percent. The minimum wage was raised the following year to $0.40. During the postwar economic boom, the minimum wage became less important until 1950, when it was nearly doubled from $0.40 per hour to $0.75 per hour. However, this wage hike's adverse impact on employment was canceled out because the Korean War erupted four months before the wage increase went into effect. The U.S. remilitarized, although this time on a smaller scale than had been the case during World War II. Large numbers of young men were once again drafted into the military. U.S. labor market conditions tightened as a result.

1956: The Feds Get Serious

The minimum wage's first significant impact on national labor market conditions occurred in 1956, when the hourly rate was raised from $0.75 to $1.00. Congress not only mandated the wage increase that

Table 4.1
EMPLOYMENT AND WAGES, 1938–1950

Year	Employment- Millions	Average Wage– Manufacturing	Federal Minimum Wage	Min. Wage as % of Avg. Wage
1938	28.9	$0.627/hour	$0.25/hour	40
1939	30.3	$0.633	$0.30	47
1940	32.0	$0.661	$0.30	45
1941	36.2	$0.729	$0.30	41
1942	39.8	$0.853	$0.30	35
1943	42.1	$0.961	$0.30	31
1944	41.5	$1.019	$0.30	29
1945	40.0	$1.023	$0.40	39
1946	41.3	$1.086	$0.40	37
1947	43.5	$1.237	$0.40	32
1948	44.4	$1.350	$0.40	30
1949	43.3	$1.401	$0.40	29
1950	44.7	$1.465	$0.75	51

SOURCE: Council of Economic Advisors (1959, pp. 164, 167). Federal minimum wages are from U.S. Department of Labor, http://www.dol.gov/whd/minwage/chart.pdf.

NOTES: Employment is total wage and salary workers in nonagricultural establishments; manufacturing wage is average gross hourly earnings in manufacturing.

year, it also authorized the U.S. Department of Labor to conduct a major survey of employers in an effort to increase compliance. Congress was serving notice that U.S. labor laws, including the minimum wage, would be more strongly enforced.

The impacts of the 1956 changes are indicated by data on U.S. unemployment rates separated by age and demographic group. Binding minimum wages have their greatest impact on teenagers because they possess the fewest marketable skills among the working-age population. Also, teens often do, or have in the past, worked at jobs easily replaceable with machinery or by conducting business in a different manner. For example, washing dishes, pumping gasoline, and busing tables in restaurants are tasks done by low-skilled workers and are replaceable through mechanization (mechanical dishwashers) or by setting up self-service operations (gas stations and fast-food restaurants).

Figure 4.1 shows the difference between the unemployment rates for white male 16-year-olds and white males ages 45-54 from 1948 to 1974. Teenagers always have higher unemployment rates than adults, but what is striking here is how the differential between the two rates expanded during the mid-1950s. It has stayed high ever since. Figure 4.2 is the same exercise,

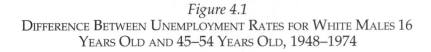

Figure 4.1
DIFFERENCE BETWEEN UNEMPLOYMENT RATES FOR WHITE MALES 16
YEARS OLD AND 45–54 YEARS OLD, 1948–1974

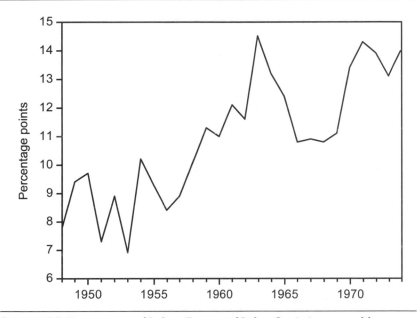

SOURCE: U.S. Department of Labor, Bureau of Labor Statistics, www.bls.gov.

this time for black male 16-year-olds and black males ages 45-54. The pattern appears again, and in this case is even more pronounced.[9] Clearly, something significant happened in the mid-1950s that severely hindered employment prospects for teenagers, and the likely candidate is the minimum wage hike combined with greater enforcement of U.S. labor laws.

A binding minimum wage creates a situation in which the pool of job applicants exceeds the number of job vacancies, which allows employers to discriminate among job seekers. Discrimination is difficult when the number of applicants is roughly equal to the number of vacancies, which is often the case when wages are determined by market forces. But a binding minimum wage creates a surplus of job applicants that allows employers to pick and choose whom to hire based on factors such as race, sex, physical appearance, and family background. Again, this discrimination would be most acute among teenagers because as the least skilled, they are most affected by the minimum wage. Figure 4.3 plots the

Figure 4.2
DIFFERENCE BETWEEN UNEMPLOYMENT RATES FOR BLACK MALES 16 YEARS OLD AND 45–54 YEARS OLD, 1948–1974

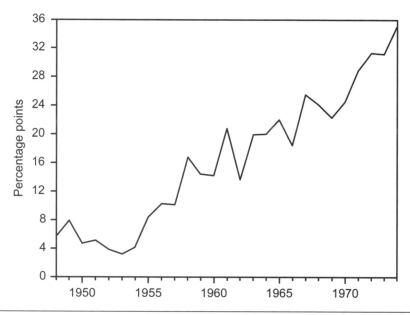

SOURCE: U.S. Department of Labor, Bureau of Labor Statistics, www.bls.gov.

difference between the unemployment rates of black and white 16-year-old males. Since 1948, rates for black teenagers have been higher than for white teenagers, in part because blacks have higher high school dropout rates. But again, what stands out here is the major change that took place in the mid-1950s. The unemployment rate for black 16-year-old males soared above the rate for same-age white males. The minimum wage is an obvious source of this change because it is highly unlikely that employers suddenly became more discriminatory against blacks in the mid-1950s than they had been in the late 1940s. Instead, the 1956 minimum wage increase created a surplus of teenagers that allowed employers to hire based on their preferences. That factor is why economist Walter Williams (2010b) calls "minimum wage laws one of the most effective tools in the arsenals of racists everywhere."[10]

Table 4.2 shows how the 1956 minimum wage change affected labor markets in the South more than in the North, and it helps explain why

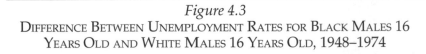

Figure 4.3
DIFFERENCE BETWEEN UNEMPLOYMENT RATES FOR BLACK MALES 16
YEARS OLD AND WHITE MALES 16 YEARS OLD, 1948–1974

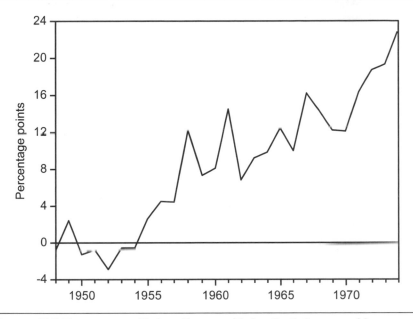

SOURCE: U.S. Department of Labor, Bureau of Labor Statistics, www.bls.gov.

northern politicians have historically been more supportive of minimum wage increases than southern politicians. In years past, a significant wage gap existed between the two regions of the country, with wages in the North being higher than wages in the South. The data in the table are average union wage rates in selected U.S. cities for two categories of low-skilled jobs: "helpers" on construction sites and "helpers" in the local trucking industries. These wage rates would have been, perhaps, 10 to 15 percent higher than the nonunion rates at the time. In 1955, the minimum wage of $0.75 was much higher in proportion to the union wage rates in southern low-wage cities than in northern high-wage cities. Then, the 1956 increase to $1.00 per hour created a situation in which the federally mandated wage was two-thirds of the union wage rates in Birmingham and Little Rock (94 percent of the union wage for trucking helpers in Birmingham), but less than 50 percent of the union rates in Chicago and Pittsburgh. In other words, the minimum wage rate had a much greater impact on local labor

Table 4.2
AVERAGE UNION WAGES (HOURLY), 1955–1956

	Building Helpers & Laborers	as % of Minimum Wage	Local Trucking Helpers	as % of Minimum Wage
All U.S. Cities				
1955	$2.16	35%	$1.85	40%
1956	$2.29	44%	$1.94	51%
High-Wage Cities				
Chicago, IL				
1955	$2.43	31%	$1.94	39%
1956	$2.58	39%	$2.04	49%
Pittsburgh, PA				
1955	$2.55	29%	$2.08	36%
1956	$2.63	38%	$2.20	45%
Low-Wage Cities				
Birmingham, AL				
1955	$1.39	54%	$1.04	72%
1956	$1.50	67%	$1.06	94%
Little Rock, AK				
1955	$1.19	63%	$1.50	50%
1956	$1.36	73%	$1.50	66%

SOURCE: U.S. Department of Labor (1975, pp. 236, 237, and 240).

market conditions in southern cities than in northern cities. Not surprisingly, federal agents investigating violations of the Fair Labor Standards Act during the 1950s found that 68 percent of minimum wage violations were in the South (Nordlund 1997, 90).

The data in Table 4.2 also help explain why increases in the minimum wage were supported by many northern politicians and business organizations, but generally opposed by southerners. Companies operating in high-wage cities compete with firms located in low-wage cities. For example, suppose that in 1955, a company operating in the South paid unskilled workers $0.75 per hour, while a company in the North that produced the same product paid its unskilled workers $1.00 per hour. The northern company could pay its workers more because they were more productive because of a higher level of mechanization. An increase in the federal minimum wage from $0.75 to $1.00 would have no impact on the wage paid to unskilled workers employed by the northern company, but it would cause a $0.25 increase in the wage paid by the firm operating in the South. In this way, labor costs would rise for the southern company but not for the northern company, giving the northern firm a competitive advantage over the southern firm. It is unsurprising, then, that northerners favored such increases.

Another aspect of the minimum wage law is that it creates strange bedfellows. During the 1950s, labor unions became strong advocates of federal price-support programs that maintain farm prices above equilibrium levels. U.S. labor leaders believed that keeping food prices artificially high would provide an incentive for farmers to continue farming instead of moving to cities where they would compete with existing workers and push down wages (Nordlund 1997, 85–86). Historically, labor interests had supported inexpensive food as a way of making laborers' wages go further.

The Increases Continue

Since the 1950s, Congress has amended the Fair Labor Standards Act several times to raise the minimum wage and expand the number of workers covered. By the early 1990s, these changes had caused the minimum wage to apply to over 90 percent of the U.S. workforce (Neumark and Wascher 1992, 55). Figure 4.4 shows the inflation-adjusted federal

Figure 4.4
INFLATION ADJUSTED FEDERAL HOURLY MINIMUM WAGE, 1938–2010

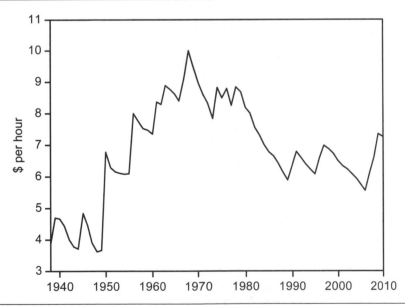

SOURCE: U.S. Department of Labor, Bureau of Labor Statistics, www.bls.gov.

minimum wage rate from 1938 to 2010. This series is calculated by dividing each year's minimum wage by the consumer price index using 2010 as the base year. For example, the $0.25 rate in 1938 is equivalent to about $4.00 at 2010 prices.

The increases during the 1950s and 1960s were substantial. By the late 1960s, the minimum wage was roughly $10.00 per hour at 2010 prices, which is a high rate when you consider that in the 1960s, workers were considerably less productive than they are today, owing to less mechanization and lower levels of technology. From the late 1960s to the late 1980s, the rate drifted down in inflation-adjusted terms, with much of that decline taking place during the 1980s. President Ronald Reagan, who occupied the White House from 1981 to 1989, did not support further increases because he believed that raising the minimum wage would discourage employment growth. As a result, the rate remained constant during his presidency (the 1981 increase was scheduled before his inauguration), which means that in inflation-adjusted terms, it fell considerably, from about $9.00 per hour to $6.00 per hour (at 2010 prices). Not coincidentally, during that decade the U.S. economy created about 18 million new jobs.

During the 1990s, the minimum wage was raised three times, going from $3.35 to $5.15, although in inflation-adjusted terms these increases were small compared with what had taken place during the 1960s and 1970s. During the 2000s, the rate was held constant until 2007, when the next set of increases began. Meanwhile, minimum wage supporters, frustrated by their failed attempts to have the rate raised during the 1980s, persuaded several state legislatures and governors to impose their own statewide minimum wages. This campaign was so successful that by 2007, 31 states had legislated minimum wage rates above the federal rate.

A Case of Bad Timing

During 2007–2009, the federal minimum wage was raised in three steps from $5.15 to $7.25, a total increase of 32 percent in inflation-adjusted terms. Although this change had no impact in states with minimum wages that remained above the federal rate (which was the case in 18 states plus the District of Columbia), it did matter in the other 32 states (Even and Macpherson 2010).

The timing of these increases turned out to be horrendous because they took place around the time of the 2007–2009 recession. Here is a timeline:

July 2007   minimum wage raised from $5.15/hour to $5.85/hour
December 2007   recession begins
July 2008   minimum wage raised from $5.85/hour to $6.55/hour

June 2009   recession ends
July 2009   minimum wage raised from $6.55/hour to $7.25/hour

The 2007–2009 Great Recession ranks as the most severe economic decline since the 1930s' Great Depression and was associated with an employment decline of 8 million jobs. Raising the minimum wage, especially the increases that took place after the recession began, constitutes poorly designed and executed economic policy.[11]

Employment conditions were extremely poor both during and after the recession, and teenagers were especially hard-hit. The unemployment rate for U.S. teenagers, which stood at 15.5 percent just before the recession began, peaked at 27.1 percent in December 2009, which is the highest rate recorded since 1948, when the federal government began reporting the series. Although it is difficult to conclude how much of that increase in teenage unemployment was due to the 2007–2009 economic recession and how much to the minimum wage increases, Even and Macpherson (2010) estimate that the wage hikes during 2007–2009 reduced national teenage employment by 2.5 percent, or about 114,000 fewer workers. These are estimates of the short-run impact; further declines are expected in the long run as employers figure out additional ways to replace workers with machines and other labor-saving methods.

So Why Does the Minimum Wage Exist?

A large body of evidence published in recent decades concludes that the minimum wage has resulted in lower levels of employment.[12] Since society presumably considers increased employment to be a desirable goal, an obvious question arises: if the minimum wage reduces employment, then why does it exist?

Remember that the minimum wage is just a government-imposed price-fixing scheme that creates winners and losers. The winners are unskilled workers with jobs at or near the minimum wage along with those who compete with those workers (who are, in many cases, members of labor unions). The losers are those who have been priced out of jobs by the artificially high wage. These losers are often teenagers, a group that does not seem to understand that the minimum wage is one of the reasons why they have poor job prospects. And even if they did understand this point, they do not constitute an effective lobbying group.[13]

Meanwhile, organized labor interests continue to lobby for higher minimum wages. They typically present their case in terms of their concern for the working poor, of the need for a "living wage." Hiding behind that argument is the fact that raising the wages of unskilled workers makes employers more likely to replace them with skilled workers who might be members of labor unions. It is essentially the same reasoning that was used to justify the original minimum wage laws in the early 1900s: raising the wages of unskilled workers (back then, it was women and children) causes those workers to be replaced by skilled workers (at the time, adult males).

Since the reality is that a significant proportion of workers actually earning the minimum wage are teenagers or young adults living with their parents, many argue that the minimum wage law doesn't actually cause much damage. Yet the effects of high unemployment among this demographic group should not be discounted. One reason is that the lack of employment opportunities for young people deprives them of valuable work experience in the form of learning the responsibility of showing up for a job on time, learning to follow directions and complete tasks, learning to work with others, and dealing with (sometimes) disagreeable bosses. These skills can prove to be beneficial later in life.

Even more pernicious, perhaps, is the result found by a number of studies that a higher minimum wage causes some U.S. teenagers to drop out of high school and instead seek jobs paying the higher wage.[14] This consequence is clearly detrimental, not just to the youths but to society as well, and certainly not what minimum wage supporters thought would happen. In addition, unemployed youths (especially males) who are not attending school are much more likely to impose costs on society by committing crimes and becoming involved in the criminal justice system.[15]

Raising unemployment, promoting racial discrimination in the workplace, increasing the high school dropout rate, and raising the incidence of crime by youths are unintended consequences of the minimum wage law. Do minimum wage advocates really support these goals?

5. The Fruits of Alcohol Prohibition: Poison Booze, Crime, and Corruption

From his mansion on Lake Shore Road in Grosse Pointe Farms, Michigan, millionaire industrialist Henry Joy had a front-row seat from which to view the U.S. government's war against illegal alcohol during the national Prohibition era. Just a few miles across Lake St. Clair and easily visible on a clear day sits Canada, a nation that did not prohibit production of alcoholic beverages. Its proximity made the area in and around Detroit, Michigan, a hot spot of activity. Southeastern Michigan and the Canadian province of Ontario are separated by a series of narrow waterways that connect Lake Huron to Lake Erie, and this geographic feature presented criminal gangs with a golden opportunity to import alcohol illegally into the United States. Smuggling Canadian whiskey and beer was a major activity in the area, and these beverages were sold throughout the Midwest.

U.S. Prohibition agents patrolled the waterways around Detroit and occasionally came upon smugglers offloading booze at Henry Joy's dock near his home. The agents would open fire if the smugglers attempted to flee, an act played out more than once on Joy's property.[1] Other events angered him as well: Prohibition agents destroyed contraband liquor on his property by breaking the bottles and then dumping the glass in the water where people swam in the summer; agents broke down the door of his boathouse while the watchman was inside and then searched the premises without identifying themselves; Prohibition agents fired rounds at a smugglers' boat out on the water and scored a hit on a passenger on a nearby excursion ship; agents shot and killed a duck hunter who ignored them, most likely because the man never heard the agents over the noise of his boat motor. Joy began referring to "the slaughter of the innocents" and worked up a laundry list of these incidents and others.[2] Joy completely lost patience with the enforcement effort and came to believe that the United States' experiment with alcohol Prohibition was a terrible mistake. He started complaining to anyone who would listen: friends, newspaper reporters, Prohibition agents, local political leaders, the governor of Michigan, all the way up the ladder to the U.S. secretary of the treasury and the president of the United States.

In 1927 he sent this telegram to President Coolidge:[3]

> President Calvin Coolidge
>
> The White House
> Washington D.C.
>
> Words cannot express my regret over your long continued apparent approval of the shootings and poisonings under the authority of the Secretary of Treasury in pursuing the futile enforcement of prohibition Stop Two recent shootings here locally of innocent law-abiding men going in small boats on their lawful occasions merely add to the long list of such atrocities under your administration Stop My hope is that this protest may aid in bringing about a cessation of unlawful searchings, seizures and killings.
>
> Henry B. Joy

The following year, he informed Treasury Secretary Andrew Mellon that "[Prohibition enforcement] conditions are a monumental disgrace to the Republican Party!!"[4] By 1929, he was so disgusted with the situation that he resigned his position with the Detroit Republican Party in protest over its support of Prohibition and received national attention for doing so. He was convinced the party was going to be ruined by its support of the issue.

This action was a complete reversal in Joy's position, because during the 1910s he had been an avid Prohibition supporter, actively involved with the Anti-Saloon League, the anti-alcohol group many consider primarily responsible for the enactment of national Prohibition in 1919. Joy believed, as many Americans did at the time, that excessive alcohol consumption was causing serious economic, social, and health problems. He also believed that urban saloons, where much of the drinking took place, were disgusting centers of vice and depravity, places where hard-working men squandered their paychecks on booze, gambling, and prostitutes. When Michigan held a referendum in 1916 asking voters if they favored imposing statewide Prohibition, Joy enthusiastically voted yes along with the majority. By the late 1920s, however, he was one of the nation's most visible and vocal critics of the law.

Henry Joy is just one example of millions of Americans whose views on alcohol Prohibition changed completely once they experienced the reality of the law. When the movement to impose alcohol bans at the state level gained momentum during the early 1900s, supporters thought they were ushering in a new era of clean living and economic prosperity that would have far fewer social problems than had been the case before. Then in 1919, when the nation took the final plunge by adopting the Eighteenth Amendment that imposed national Prohibition, supporters were ecstatic about the "Noble Experiment." Some went so far as to believe the United States would eventually be alcohol free. Their intent was, in fact, noble: to reduce alcohol consumption and many of the social ills associated with it. However, as Henry Joy and millions of others learned, the reality was very different.

The Noble Experiment lasted just under 14 years (from January 17, 1920, to December 5, 1933), but the law of unintended consequences made it an interesting and exciting 14 years. Although alcohol consumption did decline during the Prohibition era, it did not cease, which means that the social problems continued. In part, consumption didn't cease because the law had two major loopholes—home production and medicinal alcohol—which allowed legal production and consumption to continue. But a much bigger reason was a boom in illegal production and smuggling by criminals who violated the Prohibition laws. Known as "bootleggers," they realized that since the demand for alcoholic drinks was still high despite the new law, huge profits could be reaped by illegally importing the product from neighboring countries, as well as by operating their own production facilities in the United States. Profits from these illegal activities were so large that "turf wars" soon broke out as criminals committed murder and mayhem in an effort to control alcohol distribution. U.S. crime rates soared as a result. Enormous financial returns also meant that criminals had a strong incentive to keep the criminal justice system at arm's length, so corruption in the form of payoffs to public officials became an integral part of the Prohibition era. In some U.S. cities, payoffs to government officials such as mayors, police, prosecutors, and judges were so pervasive that the criminal element ended up, in effect, controlling the local government.

Meanwhile, U.S. alcohol consumers were undeniably worse off because they were paying much higher prices for considerably lower-quality beverages. And not only were those beverages low quality, some were positively dangerous. Unscrupulous operators produced and sold a significant amount of tainted alcohol, which led to several thousand deaths by poisoning, plus many times that number of disability cases, including permanent blindness. In addition, public consumption took place in illegal taverns knows as "speakeasies," and frequenting these places of businesses became a trendy activity during Prohibition, even for women, who formerly were less likely to frequent saloons. In this way, the law had the truly perverse effect of helping cause a rise in alcohol consumption by women, the very group that had been a major driving force in getting the Eighteenth Amendment ratified in the first place.

As it became increasingly apparent that the costs of Prohibition exceeded the benefits, a significant number of Americans came to agree with Henry Joy. Thus, the United States adopted the Twenty-First Amendment in 1933 ending Prohibition. The story of how the country was transformed from a group of European settlers who drank alcoholic beverages from sunrise to sunset each day to banning the substance only to make it legal again a few years later is a marvelous example of the law of unintended consequences in action.

The Beverage of Choice

The colonists who settled North America consumed alcoholic beverages in much greater quantities than Americans do today. Accounts of daily life during the 1700s suggest that it was common practice—especially among men—to begin the day with an alcoholic beverage (often alcoholic cider or rum), then consume rum during a midmorning work break, do so again during the afternoon break, drink more before and during dinner, and then consume alcohol in the evening spent at home or in a tavern. Finally, there was a "nightcap" before bed. Drinking throughout the day was both expected and encouraged for a variety of reasons, not the least of which is that few good substitutes were available. Water could be impure, and coffee and tea were expensive.[5] In addition, consumption of alcohol in moderate amounts was believed to benefit health, and people imbibed during work breaks because both employers and employees believed alcohol enhanced worker productivity. Interestingly, although a good deal of alcohol was consumed during the course of the day, its usage was spread over several hours. The consumers no doubt felt the effects, but they typically were not drunkards. In fact, drunkenness was considered socially unacceptable.

Therefore, Americans circa 1800 regularly consumed alcoholic beverages and felt no social stigma while doing so. There were critics to be sure, including the noted physician Benjamin Rush, who in the 1770s challenged the medicinal benefits of alcohol. Also, a few clergy were making the case that the substance was evil. But for the most part these arguments were ignored. Alcohol was viewed as a good, healthy substance and was widely consumed both at home and in public. People routinely toasted each other by raising drinking vessels and saying "to your health." Abstaining in social settings was considered an insult to those around you.

Rum and Corn Whiskey

In the late 1600s, slaves working on sugar plantations in the Caribbean discovered that molasses, a byproduct of sugar refining, could be fermented and then distilled into a potent brew called rum. This discovery turned out to be a major breakthrough because it led to the rise of an important industry in both the Caribbean and North America. Rum imports began to arrive in North America during the 1690s, and within a few years, the colonists were importing molasses so they could produce their own rum. The New Englanders were successful at it, and by the early 1700s were exporting rum to other countries—some to Africa in exchange for slaves who were sent to the Caribbean to produce more sugar and molasses. The resulting high supply of rum caused prices to drop. By the 1760s, rum prices were low enough that an American laborer's daily wage could purchase enough to keep him drunk for a week (Rorabaugh 1979, 64).

The onset of the Revolution changed the situation dramatically. The British navy imposed a blockade against the North American colonies, which made it difficult to import molasses. Also, since the molasses came from the British West Indies, drinking rum was considered unpatriotic. Americans were turning to substitute beverages, one of which was corn whiskey.

In those days, corn was both a major crop and a significant part of the American diet. Settlers establishing farms west of the Appalachians planted corn and were stunned by the fertility of the land, especially in the Ohio River Valley. An acre of land in that region typically yielded four times more corn than an acre in the East. Thus, as more and more farms were established in the West, corn production there soared, and the amounts harvested were well in excess of the quantity necessary to sustain the local population. Westerners began distilling the excess corn into whiskey, and by the late 1700s it was a major industry in western New York, western Pennsylvania, southwestern Ohio, and Kentucky. The beverage was being shipped throughout the United States.[6] Meanwhile, the eastern rum industry was trying to reestablish itself by once again importing molasses and distilling it into rum. But this industry's fortunes would never be the same because rum had been replaced by whiskey as the most popular distilled liquor among the middle class. The abundance of whiskey and rum on the market caused liquor prices to be low, and as the 1800s progressed, they became even lower. By the early 1820s, the price of a gallon of corn whiskey ranged from between 25 and 50 cents, which was cheap even in those days.[7]

A Nation of Drunks

Table 5.1 contains data on alcohol consumption from 1710 to 1840. The numbers in the table are gallons of pure alcohol consumed per capita for the population ages 15 years and older. In 1710, most alcohol was consumed in cider, and the predominant distilled spirit was rum. Wine consumption was low and beer was a minor beverage. The total per capita amount was 5.1 gallons that year. By the late 1700s, considerably more alcohol was being consumed, and the entire gain was in distilled spirits due to the rise of corn whiskey. As time passed, cider became less important while whiskey and rum became more important, so that by 1810, an average of 7.1 gallons of pure alcohol was being consumed by each man and woman 15 years old and older, with more than half of that amount in the form of distilled spirits.

Low liquor prices resulting from the abundance of whiskey and rum are considered to be the primary cause of the nation's drinking binge that took place during the early 1800s. By the 1820s, virtually every American celebration involved major quantities of alcohol. Funerals, weddings, holiday celebrations, public hangings, all more often than not turned into communal binges where a large proportion of the attendees drank themselves into oblivion. Election days were notable because candidates for

Table 5.1

U.S. PER CAPITA ABSOLUTE ALCOHOL BEVERAGE CONSUMPTION IN U.S. GALLONS FOR DRINKING AGE POPULATION (15 YRS+), 1710–1840

Year	Distilled Spirits	Cider	Wine	Beer	Total
1710	1.7	3.4	<.05	--	5.1
1770	3.2	3.4	<.05	--	6.6
1790	2.3	3.4	.1	--	5.8
1800	3.3	3.2	.1	--	6.6
1810	3.9	3.0	.1	.1	7.1
1820	3.9	2.8	.1	--	6.8
1830	4.3	2.7	.1	--	7.1
1840	2.5	.4	.1	.1	3.1
2005[a]	.7	--	.4	1.2	2.2

SOURCE: Rorabaugh (1979, p. 233).
[a]Data for 2005 are from Lakins, Lavallee, Williams, and Yi (2007, p. 46), with the drinking age population defined as 14 yrs+. Numbers do not sum due to rounding.

office were expected to supply all the booze the voters wanted for free, and those who didn't deliver could expect to lose the election.

These communal binges became less popular as the 1820s progressed, due in part to the temperance movement (Rorabaugh 1979, 169). But as communal binges declined in popularity, another problem arose: the solo binge, where an individual (usually male) would drink himself into a stupor, sometimes for days on end. This form of alcohol consumption was considered to be a more severe problem than communal binges because everyone would sober up after a communal binge and not do it again for a few weeks. However, men engaging in a solo binges were often unable to hold jobs and were more likely to abuse their families. This rise in solo binge drinking during the 1830s was instrumental in advancing the temperance movement.

The Early Movement

In the early 1700s, North American liquor laws were geared toward discouraging public drunkenness, restricting sales to Native Americans, and generating revenue to governments through liquor store licensing. Alcohol had its critics, but for the most part they were few and far between.[8] However, the situation began to change when rum became a common beverage because its drinkers were much more likely to become inebriated than consumers of wine and cider. Church ministers began preaching against "Demon Rum." Although most people ignored these arguments and carried on with their drinking, excessive alcohol consumption was becoming a problem, evidenced by the fact that as time passed, the liquor laws became more restrictive. Increasingly harsh penalties were being imposed for public drunkenness and sales to Native Americans.

The first significant prohibition law in North America was imposed in 1733 in the colony of Georgia. Its founder was a social reformer named James Oglethorpe, who shortly after his arrival in North America concluded that the colonists were drinking too much rum and that it was adversely affecting the condition of the colony. So he persuaded the British Parliament to impose a prohibition against importing distilled liquors into Georgia, effective in 1735. In a foretaste of what would happen nearly 200 years later under federal Prohibition, illegal stills were soon put into operation, armed bootleggers transported the liquor around the backcountry, and illegal drinking establishments became common. According to one report, government officials were pocketing large sums from the illegal trade (Asbury 1950, 21–22). In 1742, the law was declared a failure and abandoned.

The movement against excessive alcohol consumption received major support in the 1770s when well-known American physician Benjamin Rush, who signed the Declaration of Independence and later served as surgeon general of the Continental Army, questioned the medicinal affects of alcohol. He argued that although consumption in moderation was acceptable, ingesting large quantities caused severe health problems. Though these arguments are well-known today, they were considered radical at the time. Importantly, they formed a scientific basis against alcohol usage in large amounts. His 1784 pamphlet *An Inquiry into the Effect of Spiritous Liquors* was used by clergy to support their arguments regarding the evils of alcohol, and it is credited with initiating a change in American drinking habits among some members of the upper class, causing them to drink water instead of alcohol (Rorabaugh 1979, 46). However, most people ignored Rush's arguments.

Public attitudes began to change after the American Revolution, when the increase in the supply of rum and whiskey drove down prices and stimulated consumption. It became increasingly apparent that Dr. Rush's arguments about alcohol's health effects were true, and many religious leaders turned the fight against distilled liquor into a moral crusade about saving drinkers' souls from the devil. Typically at the instigation of churches, organized temperance societies were established, and though few in number during the late 1700s, they soon began to multiply. The drinking binge during the early 1800s caused a proliferation of these organizations, and in 1826, the American Temperance Society was established. Local chapters of this organization would write up a Pledge to Abstain from Alcohol and then attempt to persuade citizens to sign the agreement ("take the pledge"). By 1833, there were about 5,000 temperance organizations with total membership of 1.25 million people (Cherrington 1920, 93). That number is significant when you consider that the U.S. population in 1830 was 12.9 million.

Although the temperance societies helped cause a decline in per capita alcohol consumption during the 1830s, the problem of solo binges provided a major impetus for the movement to carry on its work. Temperance supporters advocated for statewide prohibition laws as a way to control liquor consumption, and by the 1850s, prohibition was a major political issue in the United States. Virtually every single state wrestled with it, which resulted in a flurry of legislation. Several states passed prohibition laws from 1851 to 1856, although widespread support was clearly lacking, as indicated by the fact that most of these laws were vetoed by governors, rejected by voters, ruled unconstitutional in court cases, or later repealed. By the end of the decade, the movement was losing momentum, not only because of a lack of long-term political success but also because the social reformers had shifted their focus to the slavery issue, where it would remain until the conclusion of the Civil War.

The Germans Arrive

Another factor leading to the first wave of prohibition laws was the rise of beer as a popular American drink. Before the 1840s, beer was not widely consumed in the United States because it was expensive, required skilled labor (brewmasters) to produce it, and lost its taste if not consumed within a few days. However, the situation was altered during the 1840s, when social instability in Europe's Germanic states led to a large German emigration to the United States. Sizable numbers began to arrive early in the decade, which then turned into a flood by the late 1840s. Included among these immigrants were brewmasters who knew how to produce quality beer. And at some point during the 1840s, they brought over lager yeast. This yeast was a major innovation in brewing because it produced a better-tasting beer that could be stored for a longer time. Germans were soon producing large quantities of high-quality lager beer, although during the 1840s, they were the ones drinking most of it.

Many Americans, particularly religious individuals involved with the temperance movement, were disturbed by these hard-drinking immigrants and their beer. In some U.S. cities, the Germans immigrants ignored the laws against selling or consuming alcohol on Sundays; they also tended to treat the Sabbath as a day off work to be celebrated with family, friends, and copious amounts of beer instead of attending church and spending the rest of the day quietly at home (Holian 2000, 65). Such behavior spurred on the temperance movement, especially in the Midwest, where many of these Germans immigrants were settling.

As time went on, the beverage became increasingly popular. Nonimmigrant Americans began drinking lager beer during the 1850s, and its reputation spread during the 1860s, when it was rationed out to Union army soldiers during the Civil War. Consumption was growing, although the beer industry was still relatively small and was characterized by a large number of small breweries.

Technological changes taking place during the 1870s radically altered the brewing business. Early in the decade, the great French chemist Louis Pasteur developed a process later called pasteurization that was applied to beer. It involves heating the liquid to between 130 and 140 degrees Fahrenheit, which kills bacteria but not the taste. This advancement significantly lengthened the shelf life of beer, which greatly expanded the market by allowing it to be bottled and shipped long distances. A few years later, refrigeration machines were developed. They had major applications for the brewing industry, allowing breweries to maintain temperatures low enough to manufacture beer year-round and also to ship nonpasteurized barrel beer on refrigerated railcars. Refrigeration technology also expanded demand by reducing the cost of ice, which allowed taverns to always have cold beer on hand.

These innovations, in combination with the huge U.S. population growth and urbanization taking place at the time, led to an enormous increase in the demand for beer and transformed the industry. Producers such as Anheuser-Busch and Schlitz applied these new technologies and expanded from small local companies into major national breweries. Industry output rose from just over 2 million barrels in 1863 to 13.3 million in 1880, by which time it employed thousands of workers.[9] Nicknamed "poor man's champagne," it was consumed in ever-increasing amounts because it was tasty and cheap. It also benefited from the fact that the temperance movement was focused on distilled liquor and considered beer and wine to be preferred alternatives because of their lower alcohol content. The brewing industry's output reached 40.5 million barrels by 1900, and it eventually peaked at 66.2 million in 1914.

Enter the Women

Although many temperance supporters considered beer to be a lesser evil than distilled liquor, they had very low opinions of the taverns and saloons where beer was consumed. U.S. cities, especially those with large German populations, had an abundance of such establishments, and many people viewed them as unsavory places. Saloons typically had an all-male clientele (except for prostitutes), often allowed gambling, served minors, and ignored local laws regarding hours of operation and Sunday sales. The anti-alcohol movement, which had been relatively quiet during the years leading up to the Civil War and its aftermath, considered saloons "dens of iniquity."

These concerns came to a head in December 1873, when a group of women temperance supporters in Hillsboro, Ohio, marched from their church to the local drugstores, saloons, and hotels demanding that those establishments stop serving liquor. Some retailers quickly capitulated, while others required more persuading. The women persisted, and within two months, all but a few of the town's retailers had halted sales. This successful operation led to the Women's Crusade, which started in the Midwest and then spread nationally. Groups of women would march to a saloon or other liquor retailer and demand that they stop selling alcoholic beverages. When the proprietor refused, the women would occupy the business, or gather just outside the door and drop to their knees, remaining there for hours, singing hymns and praying in an effort to persuade the owner to close down. Few drinkers wished to imbibe while this was going on; in fact, some went so far as to physically attack the women. On one occasion in Cincinnati, the women were "pelted with stones and old boots, and doused with hoses" (Holian 2000, 226). The Women's Crusade was highly effective, at least for a while. No one knows precisely how many saloons in the United States closed down as a result, but estimates run as high as 30,000 by 1875 (Asbury 1950, 85). However, the crusade did not cause any major changes in the laws permitting the saloons to operate, so once the women quieted down, many saloons reopened.

The crusade did have a long-lasting impact because it led in 1874 to the creation of the national Woman's Christian Temperance Union, which went on to play a major role in bringing about national Prohibition (the WCTU still exists). The WCTU began organizing local chapters throughout the country that stressed the reform of drunkards through God and advocated for changes in liquor laws, as well as educating the public about the dangers of drink. Increasingly, the wet-dry issue was becoming a battle of the sexes. The Women's Crusade had increased the role of women in the prohibition movement, and their influence would remain strong until the final victory in 1919.

State Constitutional Amendments

Agitation over alcohol and saloons during the 1870s resulted in the second wave of prohibition laws that were enacted beginning in the early 1880s. After the mostly hollow victories of the 1850s, the anti-alcohol interests had reached the conclusion that what were needed were laws that would stand up over time. That outcome meant state constitutional amendments because, although difficult to enact, they are hard to get rid of once in place.

The first state to adopt one was Kansas in 1880, where voters approved an amendment by a margin of about 8,000 votes, which was 4.5 percent of the total cast in the election (Bader 1986, 60). The law took effect in 1881, and the implementation law disallowed the sale of alcohol except by a druggist. Accordingly, medicinal alcohol could be purchased from a pharmacy, but only with a prescription from a physician.

Within a few years, a number of other states approved similar amendments. However, as was the case back in the 1850s, many of these victories proved fleeting because several of the new laws were gone by the end of the decade, victims of court cases or repeal. Although failing to get many lasting state Prohibition amendments passed, the prohibitionists did succeed in persuading several states to pass local-option laws, which gave local governments the right to restrict alcohol.

By the end of the 1880s, the movement was running out of gas, and one reason was poor economic conditions. A major argument advanced by the anti-alcohol forces was that Prohibition would result in a higher level of economic prosperity. Yet while states were adopting Prohibition legislation during the 1880s, economic conditions were poor, particularly for farmers. The United States suffered economic recessions from 1882 to 1885 and from 1887 to 1888. Also, the United States' return to the gold standard in 1879 set off a decline in prices that would be sustained until 1896, a condition that was especially hard on farmers because it meant that the price of their output was falling while the inflation-adjusted value of their mortgage debt was rising. Today, there is little reason to believe that Prohibition caused these national economic declines, but that is not how many saw it at the time. In their minds, Prohibition was being implemented and economic conditions were getting worse, not better.

The local-option laws put into place during the 1870s and 1880s did, in a roundabout way, help set the stage for the prohibitionists' big victory in 1919. Many of these local-option laws included large operating-license fees for saloons as a way to reduce the number of drinking establishments. Some local governments imposed license fees that ran as high as $500 to $1,000 per year, which was a huge amount of money at that time. Most small saloon operators could not afford these fees, so they turned to the breweries for help. The brewers were obviously interested in keeping saloons open because they were the primary retail outlets for beer. Anheuser-Busch, for example, purchased saloons and paid the operating-license fees, then leased the saloons back to the original owners (Plavchan 1976, 114). This move turned out to be a very important development because it gave prohibition advocates a major talking point to use in advancing their cause. Among other things, it allowed the prohibitionists to turn the battle from a war against saloons into a war against liquor manufacturers.

The Anti-Saloon League

A number of factors came together during the 1890s to make the saloons even more despicable in the eyes of the prohibitionists. Growth of beer consumption was finally slowing, due in part to continued U.S.

economic problems. The U.S. economy experienced four economic recessions from 1890 to 1900, and the demand for alcoholic beverages fell during each. Also, the United States became involved in the Spanish-American War (1898), and to help finance that conflict, the federal government enacted a series of tax increases, including a doubling of the excise tax on beer from $1 to $2 per barrel. This tax increase caused beer producers to raise prices, which further hindered consumption growth. As a result of the weak economy and rising beer prices, production and consumption were approximately flat from 1893 to 1899, which led saloons to market the beverage more aggressively.

More aggressive marketing in many low-income neighborhoods meant intensifying the practices that both encouraged drinking and inflamed the passions of the anti-alcohol forces. For example, saloons and taverns avoided the rules against Sunday sales by giving away "free" beer with the purchase of a sandwich. To attract customers, bars increasingly became involved in prostitution and gambling. They also became more likely to serve minors, and in some saloons, teenagers could be seen lined up at the bar after school. Many establishments would serve intoxicated customers, so long as they could produce the money to buy more alcohol. In addition, the economic hard times increased the number of street bums, many of whom frequented saloons. Another of the anti-alcohol forces' objections involved the practice of saloons cashing workers' paychecks. A prime location for a drinking establishment was just outside a factory's gates, and on payday, workers would head to the bar to cash their paychecks and spend some of the proceeds on alcohol. In the early 1900s, one large manufacturer in Illinois reported that of 3,600 paychecks issued on a particular payday, every single one of them was cashed in a bar (Kobler 1973, 174).

The prohibitionists viewed saloons as centers of vice and depravity. In low-income immigrant neighborhoods, most of them were dirty, foul-odored havens for drunks. The floors were covered with sawdust to soak up spilled drinks and tobacco spit from customers who missed the spittoon. Crime rates tended to be high in neighborhoods with saloons, and the sidewalks would be littered with trash and passed-out drunks. An incredibly large number of bars existed in U.S. cities, especially the ones with large German populations. For example, Cincinnati, Ohio, in 1890 had one saloon for every 37 adult males residing in the city (Holian 2000, 230). By 1899, annual beer consumption in Cincinnati was an estimated 46 gallons per man, woman, and child (Holian 2000, 209).

As far as the prohibitionists were concerned, the alcohol problem was out of control, and this was the main impetus for the formation of the Anti-Saloon League (ASL). The ASL held a national convention in 1895 where several national, state, and local temperance organizations were merged into the Anti-Saloon League of America. Since many of the ASL's officers were clergy, the ASL is best thought of as a national religious organization promoting prohibition.

The ASL was extremely formidable, in part because it was able to organize the various temperance organizations. It was also moralistic, nonpartisan, nondenominational (maintaining ties to both Protestant and Catholic churches), well financed, single-minded, ruthless, and unethical. It had one goal, which was national Prohibition, and it would pull out all the stops (allegedly including bribery) to achieve it. The ASL considered the saloons to be the liquor interests' most vulnerable point of attack, and since most were owned or controlled by breweries, the prohibitionists could blame the saloon problem on the liquor manufacturers. Funded by monthly membership dues, donations from churches, and gifts from individuals, including some deep-pocketed tycoons such as the Rockefellers, the Du Ponts, Andrew Carnegie, and Henry Ford, the ASL used these funds to hire employees whose full-time jobs were to lobby for prohibition laws. In addition, it churned out an incredible amount of printed information about alcohol. By 1912, *monthly* output from its printing plant in Westerville, Ohio, was 250 million book pages weighing about 40 tons. They included pamphlets, charts, books, newspapers, and the *Scientific Temperance Journal*. The ASL was a genuinely powerful organization, and in combination with the WCTU, it made a potent lobbying group that blamed virtually every social evil on alcohol: national disasters, venereal disease, divorce, crime, insanity, and rape (Kobler 1973, 193–95).

The ASL used its financial resources and printed message to advocate for political candidates based solely on how they would vote on the wet-dry issue. ASL officers did not care if a candidate drank or even owned a saloon (which some "dry" politicians did), nor did they care about their religious convictions. All that mattered was how they would vote on Prohibition. The ASL started out promoting local-option laws, then when alcohol restrictions had been implemented over a large area within a particular state, the next step was to advocate for a state constitutional amendment. Then, when a critical mass of states had adopted Prohibition amendments, the ASL intended to go for the grand prize of federal Prohibition.

The liquor industry fought back, but without much success. When the ASL first began complaining about the saloon problem, the brewers' response was, in effect, "what problem?" Not until the late 1890s did the manufacturers realized how serious a threat the ASL was, and they were never as well organized. Every time the ASL discovered that a politician or candidate for public office had received backing from the liquor manufacturers, he would be ridiculed as a pawn of the wets, an immoral person who favored drunkenness, drinking by children, prostitution, gambling, and so forth. Kobler notes that the ASL "could wrap itself in the robes of morality and piety" while the liquor manufacturers could not (1973, 205).

As local-option laws were applied to ever-larger areas of the country, the ASL began pushing for state constitutional amendments. Georgia was first (1907), and then the dominoes began to fall. By 1910, 13 states had adopted amendments, plus the District of Columbia, Alaska, and Puerto Rico. Another 20 states had passed laws (as opposed to constitutional amendments) imposing major restrictions on alcohol manufacturing and sales. When local-option laws are included, 95 percent of the United States' land area containing two-thirds of the U.S. population was subject to laws that either partially or completely restricted alcohol. The ASL had accomplished phase two of its three-step plan. Now it was time to go for the prize.

Toward National Prohibition

The drys believed genuine Prohibition was possible only with a federal constitutional amendment. Their reasoning was that a state could have all sorts of local-option restrictions, but as long as some areas within the state allowed alcohol, it would be an easy thing for residents of dry areas to travel to wet areas and buy booze. And even if a state passed a constitutional amendment prohibiting alcohol, neighboring states still allowed it. Of course, a flaw in the prohibitionists' logic was that the same argument applied to a country: if the United States prohibited alcohol while Canada and Mexico did not, a major smuggling industry would soon develop. Americans would travel to those countries, purchase liquor, and then try to sneak it into the United States, and profit-seeking criminals would do the same thing. The prohibitionists tended to dismiss this potential problem. Their vision, which turned out to be terribly naive, was that a national Prohibition amendment combined with strong enforcement would make the country an essentially alcohol-free zone.

Meanwhile, the dominoes continued to fall. By 1914, 9 more states had adopted constitutional amendments, and another 12 had expanded local-option laws (Kobler 1973, 205–6). That same year, the ASL scored big in the U.S. congressional elections, gaining seats for the drys in both the House and Senate. The prohibitionists made their first attempt at passing a constitutional amendment but came up short. It received a majority of votes in both the House and Senate, but not the two-thirds necessary to send the amendment to the states for ratification. Undaunted by this setback, the drys carried on with their work and reaped even more gains in the 1916 congressional elections. The prohibitionists believed that when the new Congress was seated in 1917, they had enough votes to get the amendment through.

At the time, many observers felt that the Prohibition amendment would have received the necessary two-thirds vote in 1917 regardless of external events. However, we'll never know because the process was made considerably easier by international developments. The German navy's sinking of the *Lusitania* in 1915 significantly raised anti-German sentiments in the United States, and those feelings continued to intensify to the point where in April 1917 the United States declared war on Germany and the other Central powers. This action turned out to be a huge boon to the cause of Prohibition for two major reasons: First, most of the brewers in the country were either owned or controlled by families with German names (e.g., Anheuser-Busch and Schlitz), so Prohibition became a patriotic cause because it was anti-German. Second, the prohibitionists made the argument that alcohol restrictions were important to the war effort. The claim was that foodstuffs, labor, and transportation used in the production of alcoholic beverages would be much better used to produce military supplies and feed the troops.

These factors carried considerable weight. When Congress began debating the Prohibition amendment it was a foregone conclusion that it would apply to distilled spirits. The question was whether beer and wine should be included. The brewers and vintners had long argued that their products caused considerably fewer alcohol-related problems than did distilled beverages. Therefore, their products should be exempted. The prohibitionists wanted them included. The brewers and vintners offered a compromise whereby beer and wine would be included in the amendment if it also contained a clause imposing a six-year deadline for the states to ratify. The brewers and vintners never dreamed that enough states would vote to ratify within that amount of time. The window was raised to seven years in the actual amendment.

The Eighteenth Amendment

The Hobson-Sheppard resolution submitted to Congress in 1914 formed the basis of the Eighteenth Amendment. It was drafted by the ASL and named after its congressional cosponsors, Rep. Richmond

Hobson (D-AL) and Sen. Morris Sheppard (D-TX). The 1914 version, which received a majority of yea votes but not the required two-thirds, contained Section 1:

> The sale, manufacture for sale, transportation for sale, importa-
> tion for sale, and exportation for sale, of intoxicating liquors for
> beverage purposes in the United States and all territory subject
> to the jurisdiction thereof are forever prohibited.

Note that this version prohibits alcohol for commercial uses. Home production and consumption would have been legal, as would purchasing liquor in Canada and bringing it into the United States for personal consumption or as a gift. Compare that version with the one that received the required two-thirds vote in both the House and Senate in 1917 and became Section 1 of the Eighteenth Amendment:

> After one year from the ratification of this article the manufac-
> ture, sale, or transportation of intoxicating liquors within, the
> importation thereof into, or the exportation thereof from the
> United States and all territory subject to the jurisdiction thereof
> for beverage purposes is hereby prohibited.

Unlike the 1914 version, this amendment (which superseded all state and local laws governing alcohol) could be interpreted as a blanket prohibition against producing alcoholic beverages. According to Kobler, the ASL was behind this change (1973, 210). Senator Sheppard was later quoted in the newspapers as saying he never intended to make it illegal for people to produce alcohol for their own consumption.

Section 2 of the amendment specifies that the states would assist the federal government in enforcing the law "by appropriate legislation," which referred to the enforcement law that was needed for the amendment to have any impact. In other words, alcohol was prohibited, but what would be the penalty for violating the law? A slap on the wrist or the electric chair? Or something in between? That had yet to be decided. Section 3 contained the time deadline clause for ratification by the states.

To the shock of the pro-alcohol forces, it took just 13 months for the necessary 36 states to ratify the amendment.[10] Ratification occurred on January 14, 1919. Two days later, the U.S. secretary of state announced that the constitutional process was complete and that Prohibition would take effect one year later. Ironically, this amendment, which had been partly sold as a measure to help the war effort, was approved two months after World War I ended.

The Volstead Act

The National Prohibition Act is the law that was passed on October 28, 1919, to enforce national Prohibition. This act is better known as the Volstead Act, after Representative Andrew Volstead (R-MN), who introduced the legislation (which was drafted by the ASL) to the House of Representatives on May 27, 1919.

Hearings were held a few weeks later. A major topic of discussion revolved around the definition of "intoxicating liquors" and the closely associated issue of whether or not alcoholic beer should be allowed. Distilled beverages were obviously viewed as "intoxicating" so there was never any discussion of their legality under the new law. But beer was a different story. At the one extreme, the ASL wanted to prohibit all alcoholic beverages, including beer. Its argument was that if even weak alcoholic beer was allowed, the saloons would stay open, and beer drinkers would just consume larger quantities in order to get drunk.

Others felt that beer with a low alcoholic content of around 2.5–3.5 percent should be permitted because it was nonintoxicating. This group argued that weak beer would satisfy the demands of many drinkers without causing the alcohol abuse associated with distilled beverages such as whiskey.[11] Samuel Gompers, the founder and president of the American Federation of Labor, was among those making this argument. Although he considered "prohibition by law . . . the most ineffective manner in which a temperate course may be and will be pursued by the masses of our people" (Gompers favored education programs instead), he argued that beer with 2.75 percent alcohol should be legal (U.S. Congress, Senate 1919, 6).[12] He considered this beverage to be "nonintoxicating" and "noninjurious" and believed that it was very important to the happiness of America's workers that they be allowed to enjoy beer with their lunch (U.S. Congress, Senate 1919, 9).

However, retired North Dakota Supreme Court judge Charles Pollock pointed out that allowing beer with limited alcohol content could create a new set of problems. He noted that North Dakota had already tried that approach with very poor results: "Within three months after the passage of that act we found ourselves in a horrible condition. The brewers of malt liquors made a beer containing 1.90 percent of alcohol by volume and placed therein, as a preservative, such poisons as coculus indicus, copperas, opium, extract of logwood, and many other ingredients calculated not only to make the drinker drunk, but crazy besides" (U.S. Congress, Senate 1919, 103).

In fact, negative references to the experiences in places where prohibition had already been tried were brought up more than once at the hearings. William Crounse, representing the perfume manufacturers and the wholesale druggists, warned that states that had already adopted prohibition incurred substantial enforcement costs, increased bootlegging, and experimentation with dangerous additives (U.S. Congress, Senate 1919, 117). A letter from Reverend Plard of San Juan, Puerto Rico, was entered into the record in which he described that island's experience under prohibition. Once its law was enacted, the annual demand for alcohol used in hair tonics soared from 5,000 gallons to 72,000 gallons. Realizing that this substance was ending up in beverages, the government decided to close this loophole by requiring the addition of various poisons to the alcohol. Soon afterward, physicians on the island reported a huge increase in sickness and deaths from consuming poisons (U.S. Congress, Senate 1919, 174). Samuel Gompers included a report from Detroit (author unknown) that described the situation there under Michigan's prohibition law. It included "5,000 blind pigs [illegal drinking establishments] and as many bootleggers." During the first year the law was in force, the number of arrests for drunkenness doubled, in part because "former beer drinkers have become whiskey drinkers," as prohibition created an incentive to produce and consume more potent drinks because they are easier to conceal (U.S. Congress, Senate 1919, 217). Rhode Island attorney Nathan Littlefield described what happened in his state after prohibition was instituted in 1886: "For three years this State witnessed an orgy of drunkenness and vice probably unparalleled in this country" (U.S. Congress, Senate 1919, 101).

Witnesses at the hearings also pointed out that any prohibition law could be easily circumvented because alcoholic beverages were easy to manufacture, and that bootleggers would produce much lower quality products than a legally operating industry would. In addition, Prohibition would turn normally law-abiding Americans into lawbreakers and would harm lower-income Americans much more than high-income Americans (U.S. Congress, Senate 1919, 21–22). Gompers said that he personally knew a number of rich people who had already stockpiled a lifetime's supply of booze in preparation for Prohibition.

But the Prohibition freight train was rolling, and at this late stage nothing could stop it. Congress went ahead and passed a law that differed very little from the original version introduced by Andrew Volstead. The key provisions were contained in Titles II and III. Industrial alcohol was described, as were the rules governing its manufacture and the denaturation process.[13] Fines were imposed for converting denatured alcohol back into liquor—a maximum fine of $1,000 and 30 days in prison for the first offense. The section on "Prohibition of Intoxicating

Beverages" (Title II) contained the essence of the law: "No person shall
. . . manufacture, sell, barter, transport, import, export, deliver, furnish,
or possess any intoxicating liquor except as authorized in this Act, and
all the provisions of this Act shall be liberally construed to the end that
the use of intoxicating liquor as a beverage may be prevented."

The major exceptions were medicinal alcohol and alcohol used in religious services. In a compromise clearly tilted in favor of the ASL, beer
was allowed with a maximum alcoholic content of 0.5 percent (this beverage became known as "near beer"). Thus, the law closely conformed
to the ASL's definition of "intoxicating beverages" as being anything
with an alcoholic content above zero.[14] The law also prohibited adver-
tising liquor, and manufacturing or selling any inputs used in its production (e.g., stills). Any building, boat, vehicle, et cetera, used in the
production of alcohol was a "common nuisance," and anyone using
them was guilty of a misdemeanor bearing a maximum fine of $1,000
and one year in jail. Repeat offenders could receive a maximum fine of
$2,000 and five years in jail.

The law did permit the manufacture of alcoholic beverages at home, and
the owners and their guests could legally consume the products within
that home. However, the law was violated the moment the liquor left the
property or was sold. Enforcement was to be handled by the Department
of the Treasury's Internal Revenue Bureau, and Congress appropriated
$2.1 million for that purpose for the remainder of the fiscal year (which ran
to June 30, 1920). The Treasury Department created the Prohibition Unit
(later changed to Prohibition Bureau) to carry out this task.

Congress passed the Volstead Act in October 1919, but to the surprise
of many, President Wilson vetoed it because the act included wartime
enforcement, which he no longer considered necessary. But Congress
quickly overrode the veto and the Volstead Act became law. With the
enforcement act now in place, the Noble Experiment was set to begin
on January 17, 1920.

The Inherent Problem

In 1919, the nation's collective mood was caught up with the prohibitionists, who were ecstatic over their victory, believing the new law
was going to cause a huge reduction in alcohol consumption and the
various social and economic problems associated with it. The extreme
optimists went so far as to predict that within two generations, the
United States would be alcohol free. What is striking is how little attention was being paid to the few people publically criticizing the new law.
They were arguing that the same problems that individual states had

experienced with their prohibition laws would now occur on a national scale. The prohibitionist reply was that strong enforcement would solve those problems, and that the individual states with Prohibition had not allocated sufficient resources to make their laws work.

The inherent problem was that although the ban on alcohol enjoyed wide support, a substantial portion of the population (mostly large-city dwellers) opposed it. Included among this group were many problem drinkers of course, but also immigrants from countries like France, Germany, and Italy, many of whom could never figure out why the United States wanted to prohibit alcohol; young men who considered drinking a rite of manhood; those who believed that alcohol issues should be decided by individual states and not the federal government; and individuals who felt that no government at any level should be legislating this sort of behavior. In fact, not only did a large number of Americans oppose the law, they intended to violate it.

So while the United States enacted a law prohibiting alcohol, demand had not been eliminated; the legal supply had been restricted, which was going to raise alcoholic beverage prices. Those higher prices would cause quantity demanded to fall, meaning that alcohol consumption would decline, which was the primary goal of the prohibitionists. In addition, demand would fall if the penalties for violating the new law induced many Americans to consume less. However, although alcohol consumption would fall, it would likely not decline by as much as the prohibitionists hoped because of home production and illegal sources. Moreover, demand might increase if it became fashionable to break the law. And the quality of beverages available would be significantly reduced.

In addition, a host of problems would arise due to the law of unintended consequences. First and foremost, since the liquor industry was becoming an illegal operation and because a high level of demand still existed, only a portion of which would be satisfied by legal home production and medicinal alcohol, much of the demand would be supplied from illegal sources. In other words, the liquor industry was changing from a legal business operated by distillers, vintners, and brewers who followed the standard rules of business and cared a great deal about the quality of their products and their business reputations to an illegal business where normal rules did not apply. Unscrupulous operators could enter the industry, bottle any dangerous concoction, and then glue a label on it identifying the beverage as high-quality Canadian whiskey or genuine Mexican tequila. Consumers made sick (or worse) by drinking these products were unlikely to complain to the legal authorities since doing so would be admitting that they had broken the law. (How often do you hear about users of illegal narcotics complaining to the police about product quality?) Producers could compete on price and quality as was the case when the business operated in a legal environment, but they could also attempt to improve business by using physical force to eliminate the competition. In essence, those in control of the illegal liquor industry could set their own rules, and woe be to those who did not follow them. The involvement of criminals is a large part of the reason why an enormous amount of violence took place during Prohibition, with most of it occurring within and among various criminal gangs over business deals gone bad, double-crosses, and efforts to stamp out competition.

Operating outside the law provided producers and consumers with additional incentives. Before Prohibition, liquor manufacturers conducted their operations out in the open for all to see. Their activities were legal, so they had no need to conceal production or clandestinely transport products to market. Nor did bar and saloon operators conduct business on the sly. But once the alcohol ban went into effect, there was an incentive to produce and consume physically smaller products. After all, it's much easier to hide a quart of whiskey than a case of beer. In fact, the term "bootlegging" comes from the practice of hiding a flask of liquor inside one's boot. This desire for more potent drinks created a shift in demand toward distilled beverages and away from wine and beer. That shift is another of the great ironies of Prohibition: a law designed to eliminate beverage alcohol ended up converting beer drinkers into whiskey, rum, and gin drinkers.

Since the liquor industry was now an illegal business satisfying a high level of demand, the profits turned out to be enormous. These high returns provided criminals with a strong incentive to keep the legal system at arm's length. That motivation is why corruption was such a significant component of Prohibition; criminals routinely paid off police, prosecutors, judges, and various other government officials in exchange for being allowed to conduct their activities without interference. Bootleggers considered these payoffs just a cost of doing business.

Since a large number of people would continue drinking, the Volstead Act turned vast numbers of regular Americans into criminals because they were producing and consuming illegal alcohol. A major increase in the number of criminals would lead to substantial enforcement costs. Not only would more police be needed, law enforcement agents would have to spend more of their time on alcohol violations, leaving less time for other enforcement activities. Furthermore, the number of court cases would increase, and more convictions meant more prisoners housed at taxpayers' expense. Before Prohibition went into effect, supporters were aware that enforcement costs would be incurred to administer the Volstead Act, but they argued that the resulting fall in alcohol consumption would cause such large declines in other alcohol-related social problems that overall costs to society would fall.

Another outcome that should have been obvious to anyone who gave it much thought was that Prohibition would create a strong incentive to smuggle liquor into the United States from neighboring countries. Since most alcohol demand would now be satisfied by low-quality output from home production and moonshining, quality liquors would fetch a huge premium. The neighboring countries of Canada (whiskey and beer), Mexico (tequila and beer), and the Caribbean nations (rum) were well positioned to satisfy this demand. The actual importation was handled by criminal gangs, which purchased the liquor in the foreign countries and then transported it to the United States, where they could sell it at a tremendous profit. This smuggling was a major criminal activity in border areas, especially along the U.S.-Canadian border.

The prohibitionists were no doubt correct that a large-enough enforcement program might have caused Americans to follow the law to the letter and would thereby have virtually eliminated illegal alcohol, but at what cost? An enforcement effort of this magnitude would have required police patrolling every single mile of the nation's coastline and international borders and close monitoring of all suspected criminals, as well as the 30–40 percent of the adult population who wanted to consume illegal alcohol. In addition, severe penalties for offenders who were caught and convicted would have been necessary. The cost to the taxpayers of carrying out this level of enforcement, the number of employees required, plus the huge infringement on personal freedoms would have been enormous. So yes, with a large-enough level of enforcement, Prohibition could have largely eliminated illegal alcohol. But Americans, many of whom opposed the law from the start, simply were not willing to incur anything even approximating that level of costs.

Satisfying Demand

When the law took effect on January 17, 1920, the following sources were available to satisfy the demand for alcoholic beverages:

Home Production

Alcoholic beverages are easy to manufacture; the difficult part is producing ones that taste good. But by making them at home from known ingredients, consumers at least knew their drinks were safe, which is more than could be said about beverages purchased from moonshiners.

Home-produced wines were popular, especially among Americans of southern European descent who were concentrated in cities in the East and Midwest. Ironically, U.S. winemakers thought that Prohibition was going to put them out of business. But, in fact, many thrived during the 1920s because vintners not only make wine, they also grow grapes, and demand for this fruit soared because of all the winemaking going on in homes. Within five years of Prohibition, the number of acres of California land allocated to grape production increased sevenfold (Kobler 1973, 240). According to official statistics presented to the U.S. Senate in 1931, California grape production roughly doubled from 1920 to 1928 (U.S. Congress, Senate 1931, vol. 1, 128). Grape-growing also boomed in the Great Lakes states. Even though supply increased substantially, demand went up even more, which is reflected in prices: for example, California vintners Ernest and Julio Gallo mention in their autobiography that just before Prohibition, grapes sold for $5 to $7 per ton, then reached $120 per ton while the alcohol ban was in place (1994, 16). Not only was Prohibition good for the grape business, sales of the tools used to make wine, such as bottles, corks, and presses, also boomed.

Beer was another popular beverage. The necessary ingredients for a basic beer are malt extract, hops, sugar, and yeast, all of which were readily available in grocery stores. Meanwhile, thousands of retail outlets were established that specialized in selling those ingredients plus equipment, such as crocks and bottle caps. The 1931 U.S. Senate report estimated that based on hops production, U.S. output of home brew during the fiscal year from July 1, 1929, to June 30, 1930, was 683 million gallons, accounting for 23.2 million gallons of absolute alcohol (U.S. Congress, Senate 1931, vol. 1, 129). The U.S. population in the 1930 census was 123 million.

The major distilled beverage produced in American homes was called bathtub gin. A simple version involved heating corn mash on the stove, in a pot covered by a towel. Alcohol boils (at 180–200 degrees Fahrenheit) before water, so heating it to a temperature high enough to create alcohol vapors but low enough to prevent the water from boiling allowed the home-producer to collect the alcohol in the towel. The towel was then wrung out and the liquid used as the base for the gin. When a sufficient quantity of alcohol was collected, it was mixed with water, glycerin, and juniper oil, and then bottled. The beverage was potent but unsavory, so it was typically mixed with fruit juice or some other beverage before drinking. More sophisticated alcoholic beverages could be produced with a still, and small stovetop models were available for a few dollars apiece.

Thus, millions of U.S. households produced alcoholic beverages for their own consumption. Several observers during those times describe a stench permeating many urban neighborhoods from all the home production taking place. And in 1928, city officials in Tarrytown, New York, had to appeal to residents to stop flushing their leftover mash into the sewer system because it was getting plugged up from "grain, potato peelings, and all matter of material from base products used to make alcoholic beverages, including prune pits" (Boardman 1988, 95).

Illegal Imports

If anyone should have been rooting on the U.S. prohibitionists, it was the liquor manufacturers in Canada, Mexico, and the Caribbean. Few had more to gain because their U.S. competitors were going to be denied the right to produce alcohol. Furthermore, since Prohibition would reduce the quality of alcoholic beverages being produced in the United States, there would be a premium on quality drinks, and producers in neighboring countries were in a strong position to supply the market. They could continue to produce in their own countries because it was legal to do so, and they could sell to whoever wanted to buy. It wasn't the foreign manufacturers' problem if their alcoholic beverages ended up in the United States.

Canadian whiskey and beer manufacturers were especially big winners from U.S. Prohibition because they possessed two major advantages: (1) many of their distilleries and breweries were located in Ontario and Quebec, so they were physically close to a huge segment of the U.S. market; and (2) they produced high-quality products. Thus, much of the smuggling into the United States occurred along the U.S.-Canadian border, especially in Michigan and New York. Two other hot spots were "rum row" along both the Atlantic Coast and Gulf of Mexico, where Caribbean rum was smuggled in, and the U.S.-Mexican border towns in Texas and California, where tequila and beer were brought in.

As Henry Joy was well aware, geography made the area in and around Detroit, Michigan, a particularly lively place. Detroit is separated from Canada by the Detroit River, a body of water about a half mile wide and featuring several islands, about half of which are owned by each country. It was legal for an American to cross over to Windsor, Ontario, buy whiskey and beer, and then load it onto a boat for shipment. Canadian customs officials required a form identifying where the shipment was bound for, but the stated destination was not binding.[15]

Of course, the Canadians knew exactly what was going on, but why would they raise a fuss? As far as they were concerned, this was a fabulous arrangement: their farmers enjoyed a high demand for grains used to produce the whiskey and beer, and the booming distilling and brewing businesses provided jobs for Canadians and tax revenue for their government. During the 1920s, output of Canadian distilleries quadrupled and liquor taxes collected by the Canadian government rose sixfold (Brown 1994, 97–98).[16]

As long as the smugglers stayed in Canadian territory, the U.S. border patrol could not touch them.[17] If the border patrol was in sight, the smugglers could land on a Canadian island and wait for the border patrol to leave before continuing the crossing. In some cases, even if the border patrol was in sight it was not a problem because the agents were receiving payoffs in exchange for allowing the liquor into the country. A huge amount of corruption occurred at this border; U.S. border patrol agents actually worked out a price schedule for the smugglers: 29.5 cents per case of beer, $1.87 per case of whiskey, and occasional "free nights" where the border patrol would ignore all shipments across the river in exchange for a lump-sum payment. Corrupt officials even offered rebates to smugglers who identified other smugglers who had moved liquor across the river without paying the fee.[18] The 1931 Senate report naively characterized the situation at Detroit as follows: "Apparently there has been a bad condition of stupidity or demoralization among American officials at that port" (U.S. Congress, Senate 1931, vol. 1, 26).

Tapping Existing Inventories

The production of quality whiskey includes an aging process to enhance its taste, in which the whiskey is stored in wooden barrels for a period of years. Beginning in the late 1890s, distilleries began storing some of this whiskey in warehouses operated under the supervision of the U.S. government. The original purpose of this arrangement was so the federal government could guarantee the whiskey's authenticity.[19] This system became popular over time, and when national Prohibition went into effect in 1920, a considerable amount of this whiskey was in storage, around 62 million gallons. The federal government intended this whiskey to be sold as medicinal alcohol (U.S. Congress, House 1920, 7).[20]

The medicinal alcohol system typically worked as follows: A patient with a prescription from a physician would purchase whiskey from a druggist who had bought it from a drug wholesaler. The wholesaler acquired it from the owner of the whiskey (sometimes, but not always, the original producer) who was storing it in a bonded warehouse. Although the total amount of alcoholic beverages derived from this source was small compared with home production and moonshining, the bonded whiskey–medicinal alcohol system was notable for its multiple opportunities for fraud. A basic problem was that the bonded whiskey was worth significantly more on the black market than it was on the legal medicinal market, which the criminal element was quick to recognize. Bonded whiskey was, in fact, liquid gold.

The first place where mischief could occur was at the bonded warehouse, and the problems were serious enough that Congress held hearings on this issue a month after Prohibition went into effect. The problem was theft. And a major weakness in the system was that there were over 350 bonded warehouses, several of which were in remote areas, and 450 federal employees to monitor them. Between July 1919 and February 1920, 88 known thefts occurred from the bonded warehouses, and others came to light later when investigators discovered that some of the barreled whiskey in the warehouses had been replaced with liquids such as denatured alcohol (U.S. Congress, House 1927, 57). Congress discussed consolidating the whiskey into fewer warehouses so as to be better able to guard them, but that was not done until the late 1920s. By then, so much of the bonded whiskey was gone, either legitimately withdrawn or stolen, that Congress was authorizing distilleries to produce 2 million gallons of whiskey per year for the medicinal market in order to replenish inventories.[21]

Legal ownership of this bonded whiskey was held through a "withdrawal certificate," which entitled the owner to withdraw whiskey from the bonded warehouse. These certificates could be bought and sold in the marketplace. And when the whiskey was withdrawn from the warehouse, a tax was owed to the federal government, the amount depending on the alcohol's intended use. If it was for beverage purposes (i.e., medicinal alcohol), the tax was $6.40 per gallon; if it was for nonbeverage purposes (e.g., scientific experiments or as an input into a nonbeverage product, the tax was $2.20 per gallon. If the alcohol was denatured before it left the warehouse, there was no tax. Prohibition officials tried to monitor this process very closely because sizable tax revenues were involved, and the situation was rife with potential fraud. For example, whiskey leaving the warehouse for "nonbeverage" purposes at the lower tax rate might end up being used as beverage alcohol instead.

Once the whiskey left the warehouse, all sorts of things might happen. It could get stolen, or if it made its way to the wholesale druggist, there was an incentive to dilute it with water or something dangerous. The same things could occur when the liquid reached the retail druggist, who might also dilute the product. In the end, the consumer of medicinal alcohol was almost always purchasing a product much inferior to the original that left the bonded warehouse.

A man named George Remus was among the first to realize that huge profits could be earned from these inventories, and his story illustrates some of the shortcomings of the program. When Prohibition went into effect, Remus was earning his living as a criminal defense lawyer in Chicago, and he soon found himself defending bootleggers being prosecuted for violating the Volstead Act. Remus realized that the profits in the illegal alcohol business were larger than what he was earning as a lawyer, so he began to consider changing to a more lucrative career.

Remus did some research and learned that most of the bonded whiskey, which was typically stored near the distilleries that produced it, was located within a few hundred miles of Cincinnati, Ohio (most of the bonded whiskey was in Kentucky and Pennsylvania). So he relocated to that city, bringing with him seed money of about $100,000, and promptly began approaching the distillery owners with title to those bonded whiskey inventories to see if they wanted to sell their holdings.[22] These distillers were a discouraged group because Prohibition had shut down most of their production. And since they lacked the criminal mind of a man like George Remus, they did not see the possibilities they were holding in their hands. Remus was able to purchase many of the certificates for $150 apiece (which entitled the owner to withdraw 100 gallons), which meant he was paying $1.50 per gallon (Lindsay 1974). With the $6.40 tax added on, Remus's cost was $7.90 for each gallon withdrawn from the bonded warehouses. In effect, Remus was purchasing distilleries' inventories for fire-sale prices, because the inventory could be sold at black-market prices of $25 per gallon or more.

His next step was to set up a drug wholesaling operation. His legal front was to sell his bonded whiskey to his wholesaling company, which would then sell it to retail druggists. The operation as Remus initially set it up was legal, and he likely would have earned high profits if he had kept the operation legitimate. But he had grander plans. Rather than sell the whiskey on the legal market as medicinal alcohol, he wanted to sell it at the higher prices on the black market.

He accomplished this feat in a variety of ways. One method was to have his employees "hijack" the whiskey he owned while it was being transported from his own bonded warehouse to his drug wholesale company. He could report to the government that it had been stolen, so it need never appear on the medicinal market. Another scam (for which he eventually ended up in court) involved secretly running a hose from a bonded warehouse to the outside so he could pump his own whiskey from the building. This way he avoided the $6.40 per gallon tax. Much of the bonded whiskey he absconded with was moved to a farm he owned outside Cincinnati, where it was then shipped off to the black market in various states throughout the Midwest. His business employed 3,000 people, operated in eight states, handled about 3 million gallons of booze, and grossed somewhere between $60 million and $75 million, from which he paid around $20 million in bribes to a large number of police and U.S. Treasury agents (Lindsay 1974). These activities earned him the title King of the Bootleggers. One of his better-known transactions (because it resulted in a criminal trial) involved spending $125,000 to purchase 891 barrels of whiskey at the Jack Daniel's distillery in Missouri, which works out to about $3.30 per gallon.[23] He sold the whiskey for $25–$30 per gallon (Asbury 1950, 221).[24] Over the course of his criminal career, Remus is estimated to have amassed a personal fortune of $20 million.[25]

Although Remus is the most famous character who exploited the bonded whiskey–medicinal alcohol feature of the Prohibition laws, many others were doing similar things on a smaller scale. In fact, the entire system was fraudulent. Even the special government prescription certificates necessary to purchase medicinal alcohol somehow ended up in the hands of criminals who then sold them to the public, pre-signed by a supposed physician.

According to the federal government's records, withdrawals from bonded warehouses peaked at 8.7 million gallons in 1921, then settled in the range of 1.5–2.0 million gallons per year until the late 1920s (U.S. Congress, Senate 1931, vol. 1, 27). It is unclear how much of that whiskey ended up being sold in its original form to prescription holders needing medicinal alcohol for their various physical ailments, but it was probably a very small proportion of the total. Although medicinal alcohol was minor compared with the total amount being consumed from all sources during Prohibition, it is notable because it allowed access to the American "good stuff," and by doing so presented a major opportunity for crime and corruption.

Moonshining: Illegal Production for Sale on the Black Market

The major source of the alcoholic beverages sold on the black market, in speakeasies, on street corners, in backrooms, and elsewhere was production by moonshiners. These operations ranged from large-scale, sophisticated facilities with modern equipment to rank amateurs operating stills in hidden or remote locations. The quality of moonshine ranged from acceptable to poisonous, with most of it near the lower end of the scale.

This clandestine production took place anywhere and everywhere, in homes, barns, remote rural locations, abandoned commercial buildings, and former breweries and distilleries that had supposedly shut down but were instead operating illegally and were protected from the law by bribery payments. In some cases, production took place in legally operating breweries that were producing "near beer." This weak version of beer involves producing regular beer and then removing most of the alcohol. This situation presented a tempting profit opportunity, so some breweries produced near beer for the legal market when Prohibition agents were monitoring the situation, and regular beer for the black market when the agents were gone or had been bribed. The 1931 Senate report concluded that "a large percentage of these plants [were] now probably violating the national prohibition act" (U.S. Congress, Senate 1931, vol. 2, 125). In most cities, the moonshining business was managed by criminal gangs. Chicago's "Terrible" Genna brothers paid hundreds of people a daily wage of $15 to manufacture alcohol in their homes. Gang members would routinely pass through neighborhoods and collect the alcohol (which was stored in a warehouse located four blocks from a police station) before sending it off to the speakeasies.[26]

Many moonshiners were just amateur operators making alcoholic drinks in squalid conditions. Government agents were busy tracking these people down, and while doing so broke up thousands of stills and discovered all sorts of bad production techniques. During fiscal year 1929, authorities seized 15,730 distilleries, 11,416 stills, and 1.14 million gallons of liquor (U.S. Congress, Senate 1931, vol. 1, 23). Some moonshiners used old automobile radiators to condense the alcohol vapors. Radiators have lead in them, so this method subjected consumers to potential lead poisoning. Prohibition agents in Pittsburgh discovered a brewery operation inside a former slaughterhouse. The beer was being fermented in vats that had previously been used to dip pig carcasses before skinning (Kobler 1973, 248). Prohibition Unit agents in Texas caught a moonshiner producing alcohol in the yard of a fertilizer factory, using garbage as mash and doing this three feet from the carcass of a dead horse (Haynes 1923, 192). Asbury notes that "it was not uncommon for prohibition agents to find in the cooking and fermenting vats, especially in the tenements, chunks of bone, decayed meat and other garbage, and carcasses of rats, cats, and mice, with dead cockroaches and other insects floating on top of the mash" (1950, 277).

Moonshiners also converted industrial alcohol into beverage alcohol, which is where much of the genuinely nasty stuff came from. When Prohibition took effect, the government could not shut down the entire alcohol-producing industry because there were (and still are, of course) many other uses for the product besides potable beverages. The same alcohol used in beverages was used in various food products, as well as serving as an input in scientific experiments. More important in terms of magnitude were the many industrial uses. For example, the booming automobile industry had increased the demand for antifreeze, which contains alcohol. In addition, alcohol served as a component in various cleaning compounds, wood conditioners, and several personal sundry items, such as cosmetics, perfume, and after-shave lotion. Years before Prohibition was enacted, nonbeverage alcohol had been exempted from federal taxes, but only if it were denatured (i.e., rendered unfit for human consumption through the addition of chemicals). There were several government-approved denaturing formulas, some of which involved the addition of wood alcohol. For example, formulas No. 1 and No. 3-A both required the addition of 5 gallons of wood alcohol (methyl alcohol) to every 100 gallons of beverage alcohol (ethyl alcohol). Wood alcohol is a poison that can cause blindness and death; once mixed into beverage alcohol, the two are difficult to separate.

According to the Prohibition Bureau, industrial alcohol cost $0.38 per gallon to produce and sold for about $0.50 (U.S. Congress, Senate 1931, vol. 2, 116).[27] Meanwhile, depending on local supply and demand, a gallon of moonshine could sell for $10 or more. So huge profits were to be made for those willing to convert denatured alcohol into beverage alcohol by attempting to separate out the poisonous chemicals. They would purchase denatured industrial alcohol under phony pretenses and then attempt to redistill it by boiling off the ethyl alcohol. Problems arose because some of the poisons would remain with the alcohol, especially if the operator was not careful (and most were not) about capturing the alcohol vapors at precisely the right temperatures. If the moonshiner captured the vapors at temperatures just before alcohol's boiling point ("the heads") or just beyond ("the tails"), poisons could leave with the alcohol. Sometimes bootleggers would conduct the procedure twice, but the end product still contained poisons. In fact, some moonshiners didn't even bother trying: "Around New York [bootleggers] were employing what the [prohibition] agents called the cold process, namely, mixing formula 3-A [which contained wood alcohol] directly with coloring or flavoring and other alcohol" (U.S. Congress, Senate 1931, vol. 2, 332). It was then sold as beverage alcohol.

The result was a huge amount of tainted booze on the black market that caused thousands of deaths and countless more cases of permanent disability. It is impossible to know just how much redistilled and un-treated denatured industrial alcohol ended up being consumed as bev-erage alcohol, but it was surely enormous. One hint can be ascertained by the production of "specially denatured" alcohol. This category did not contain wood alcohol, so it was the type moonshiners were most likely to distill into beverage alcohol. Legal production of specially de-natured alcohol soared during the 1920s, from 9.9 million gallons in 1921 to 54.5 million gallons by 1929 (U.S. Congress, Senate 1931, vol. 1, 23). Although a great deal of that increased output went for industrial uses in the booming U.S. economy, a significant amount ended up in the hands of moonshiners. Perhaps the best evidence of the pervasive-ness of this problem is provided by the results of chemical tests the Prohibition Bureau conducted on liquor seized in raids on moonshin-ing operations and illegal drinking establishments. Test results from 1923 to 1927 showed that nearly 99 percent of contraband liquor seized contained chemicals used in denaturants (Kobler 1973, 399).[28]

The precise number of deaths that resulted from poisoned alcohol is unknown, but it probably numbered in the tens of thousands.[29] Mean-while, there were many more victims of disabilities caused by bad booze. One of the more famous cases was the early 1930s' outbreak of "jake foot" that occurred when several thousand people in U.S. cities consumed a chemical compound called tricresyl phosphate, which had ended up in fluid extract called Jamaica ginger (commonly referred to as "jake"). Jamaica ginger was a prescription remedy (containing 90 percent alcohol) for stomach ailments, yet in several states it was sold over the counter (Kobler 1973, 302). Apparently, a large batch was made from denatured alcohol and hit the market laced with tricresyl phosphate, which can cause permanent nerve damage. Jake foot was the name given to the victims' condition, which caused them to walk toe first, then with the heel hitting the ground hard. Wichita, Kansas, was especially hard-hit. By the summer of 1930, there were 500 victims, which constituted about 1 percent of the town's male population.

Did Prohibition Reduce Alcohol Consumption?

The evidence suggests that alcohol consumption did decline during Prohibition, which is to be expected because restricting legal supply put upward pressure on prices. In addition, the fact that quality had seriously deteriorated further reduced demand. At the time, many noted the fall in consumption while acknowledging that calculating the actual amounts was extremely difficult because so much of the production was coming from unmeasured sources.[30]

An economist named Clark Warburton used data he considered reliable to estimate alcohol consumption during Prohibition. He employed a series on output of agricultural goods used in alcohol production (e.g., grapes and hops), arrests for drunkenness, and deaths caused by alcoholism. Many believe his results are reasonably accurate; they are shown in Figure 5.1, which plots U.S. per capita consumption of pure alcohol from 1900 to 1929 (Warburton did not supply an observation for 1920). When the series begins in the early 1900s, U.S. alcohol consumption was well below its peak, which had occurred around 1830 (when it was 7.1 gallons per capita!), and stayed within the range of about 1.4 to 1.8 gallons per capita until 1918, when it plummeted. Congress passed the Food Control Bill as a war measure in September 1917, which prevented

Figure 5.1
U.S. PURE ALCOHOL CONSUMPTION, 1900–1929

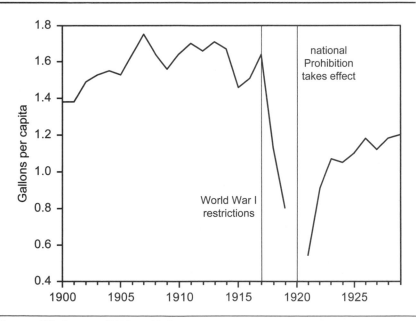

SOURCE: Warburton (1932, p. 224).

foodstuffs from being distilled into liquor. Then in December, President Wilson ordered a 30 percent reduction in foodstuffs available to brewers and prohibited producing malt liquors stronger than 2.75 percent alcohol. In 1918, more restrictions were imposed that moved the beer industry toward a shutdown by the end of the year. By 1919, per capita consumption was about half of what it had been in 1916. Then in 1920, the Eighteenth Amendment and the Volstead Act took effect, and alcohol consumption bottomed out at 0.54 gallons per capita in 1921.

Alcohol consumption soon rebounded, however, although not to the levels reached before World War I. It took criminal operators a few years to get their production and importing operations up and running, plus the public needed time to discover various ways to violate the law. This pattern is consistent with the prices of alcoholic beverages: a magazine that reported the prices of drinks served at New York speakeasies shows that shortly after Prohibition, prices rose as much as 400 percent, but over time they drifted back down (Kobler 1973, 224).

By 1925, consumption was about 65 percent of pre-Prohibition rates, and just over 70 percent by 1929.[31] Warburton's results are underscored by data from a study by the Metropolitan Life Insurance Company of its policyholders:

Year	Deaths per 1,000 from Alcoholism
1911	0.040
1919	0.014
1920	0.006
1928	0.033
1929	0.034

Source: U.S. Congress, Senate (1931, vol. 1, 31).

Here again, the pattern suggests that a major decline in consumption took place during the first years of Prohibition, followed by an increase, but with levels staying below what had been the case before Prohibition was enacted. The company attributed the increase after 1920 not only to the rebound in consumption but also to the "greater toxicity" of alcohol from illegal sources, such as denatured alcohol.[32]

Arrests for drunkenness (shown in Figure 5.2) is another good proxy for alcohol consumption, and once again the evidence suggests that alcohol consumption declined significantly in the late 1910s and early 1920s, then rose , although staying short of the levels that existed before Prohibition (*Wickersham Report* 1931, 216).[33]

Therefore, Prohibition was hugely successful at causing a major decline in alcohol consumption *initially*, although the lasting effects were

Figure 5.2
ARRESTS FOR DRUNKENNESS PER 10,000 POPULATION
IN 383 U.S. CITIES, 1910–1929

SOURCE: Warburton (1932, pp. 101, 102).

considerably less. By the late 1920s, per capita alcohol consumption was below its pre–World War I level, but Americans were still consuming the beverages in vast quantities.[34] Prohibition supporters were hugely disappointed and blamed it on weak enforcement.

Enforcement, Crime, and Corruption

The public was split regarding the Eighteenth Amendment and Volstead Act. At one end of the spectrum were ardent prohibitionists who felt that state and local governments should vigorously enforce the law; they were chronically disappointed with what they considered a weak, underfunded effort by government. They wanted considerably more money spent to hire additional enforcement agents to ferret out the bootleggers and moonshiners. At the opposite end were those who, for a variety of reasons, opposed the entire Prohibition effort. As far as they were concerned, the Eighteenth Amendment should never have been ratified, and *any* enforcement effort was too much. The federal government took the usual path of compromise, and by doing so pleased virtually no one. Prohibition was enforced, but nowhere near the quantity of resources necessary to put a serious dent in the illegal alcohol trade were used. Yet the effort was enough to make life miserable for some of the producers and consumers who were caught, and to push the liquor business underground as an illegal activity in many places. This push into illegality led to a huge amount of crime and corruption, which was precisely opposite of what the prohibitionists had promised would happen. It was a major reason why Prohibition eventually lost public support.

When the law went into effect in January 1920, the federal government created the Prohibition Unit, which was charged with enforcement. By June 30, the agency employed 2,483 people, of which 1,493 were enforcement agents.[35] That number translates into about one federal enforcement agent per 70,000 Americans. Most of the agents were paid $1,680 annually, which was not a large salary at that time, especially for those living in cities.[36] These low salaries became an issue early on because they were blamed for high employee turnover, and also for making agents more likely to accept bribes. Two other organizations involved in the effort were the Coast Guard and Customs Bureau, both of which focused on intercepting liquor being smuggled into the country.

The enforcement operation was slapped together rather quickly in 1920. A Senate report would later describe the initial hiring of agents as being carried out in "a haphazard, indiscriminate method . . . unregulated by any civil-service requirements" (U.S. Congress, Senate 1931, vol. 2, 210). Problems quickly surfaced in the form of turnover, with some of it due to dismissals of corrupt agents. During the first six months, the turnover rate among enforcement agents was 15 percent, followed by a whopping 101 percent during fiscal year 1921. Roughly 8.5 percent of the personnel in 1921 were dismissed "for cause," which included "bribery, extortion, theft, violation of the National Prohibition Act, falsification of records, conspiracy, forgery, [and] perjury" (*Wickersham Report* 1931, 30).

Major changes were finally made in 1927 when Congress abolished the Prohibition Unit, replaced it with the Prohibition Bureau, and required enforcement agents to meet civil service requirements. Agents now had to take written and oral examinations, and existing personnel did not fare well under this new system: only 30 percent passed both examinations. Not surprisingly, this piece of information received major coverage in the newspapers and proved hugely embarrassing to the Prohibition Bureau. The new hiring system did lead to a substantial decline in employee turnover, but corruption continued.

Federal funding for enforcement increased substantially during the 1920s, but it was always a drop in the bucket compared with the amount necessary to cause a significant restriction in the supply of illegal liquor. By fiscal year 1930, federal spending for enforcement was over $13 million, and the Prohibition Bureau had roughly twice as many employees as it had in 1920 (U.S. Congress, Senate 1931, vol. 2, 208, 216–19). From 1920 to 1930, federal expenditures allocated to enforcement totaled almost $112 million.

Although these amounts were large at the time, they still represented a paltry share of total federal spending. For example, in 1929 the federal government spent $1.36 billion (in 1929 dollars), which means that the funding for Prohibition enforcement that year (about $13 million) was 0.00956 of the total, or 0.956 percent of federal spending.[37] Clearly, it was not at the top of the list of federal government priorities. To cite just one example of what these numbers meant operationally, during 1925 the federal government had a grand total of 170 Customs Bureau personnel and 110 Prohibition Unit agents monitoring the 3,700 miles of U.S. borders with Canada and Mexico (*Wickersham Report* 1931, 25).

The enforcement effort wasn't high on many states' priority lists either, a source of frustration for both the prohibitionists and federal enforcement officials. When the Eighteenth Amendment was ratified, the Anti-Saloon League was well aware that Prohibition might fail if states did not make a concerted effort in harmony with the federal government. However, enforcement efforts by the various states ran the gamut from strong to virtually nonexistent. Kansas apparently made a serious effort, and the ASL mentioned that state as a model of what could be accomplished, although widespread public support for Prohibition in Kansas certainly helped (Bader 1986, 203). However, in many other states the situation was different, especially by the late 1920s, by which time Prohibition had lost a great deal of support.

Reliable data on state and local government enforcement efforts do not exist, but there is plenty of casual evidence to indicate that in many places, either the laws were not being enforced at all or the police were making just a token effort to assure both the public and federal authorities that they were at least going through the motions. In some smaller towns, the local police did not enforce the law, because they didn't agree with it, they were being paid off, or they feared retaliation from the bootleggers. Small-town police were also poorly paid, making them more vulnerable to corruption, and they often owed their jobs to prominent locals who were involved in the illegal liquor trade.[38] In fact, the 1931 Senate report refers to cases where "local police openly have been antagonistic to the Federal enforcement officers, to the extent in some cases of aiding and abetting assaults on these officers" (U.S. Congress, Senate 1931, vol. 2, 179).

In many cities, the liquor laws were largely ignored because they had so little public support. Criminal gangs were strongest in these localities because of the substantial demand for alcohol, so the exceptional financial returns provided them with a strong incentive to bribe police and other local government officials to allow the gangs to operate without legal interference. New York City, Detroit, and Chicago are just three examples of cities with thousands of illegal drinking establishments. A police official in Detroit claimed that city had at least 15,000 such establishments, and the estimate for New York City was in the neighborhood of 32,000.[39] The police, of course, knew the locations of these operations and were often customers. Kobler quotes a New York journalist explaining why Prohibition enforcement agents were despised in that city: "It was a common sight in New York speakeasies to see a group of agents enter a place at noon, remain until almost midnight, eating and drinking, and then leave without paying the bill" (Kobler 1973, 272). Police would make an occasional liquor raid (often against an operator who had not been paying bribes) to show the local prohibitionists and the federal government that they were, in fact, enforcing the law. But often another purpose of these raids was to serve notice to the criminal element of what might happen if bribes weren't paid.

The advent of Prohibition presented organized crime with an unprecedented economic opportunity. Criminal gangs would procure liquor and then sell it in retail outlets (e.g., speakeasies) that they either owned or controlled. If any competition appeared in their territories, they would try to eliminate it by violent means in order to ensure their stream of monopoly profits. Illegal liquor also allowed them to combine their bootlegging activities with the gambling and prostitution operations by serving their illegal booze in gambling halls and brothels.

To observers at the time, the heightened fortunes of organized crime and the associated effects on local governments were among the more tragic features of the Prohibition era. The Eighteenth Amendment and Volstead Act allowed a group of "two-bit hoods" to become multimillionaires, and while doing so allowed organized crime to extend its tentacles throughout many governments. The corruption was pervasive, reaching from street cops to mayors, and then on to county and even state officials.

To cite just a few examples of many, Chicago's Genna brothers were paying off 400 policemen each month, as well as bribing police captains, detectives, and all the way up the hierarchy to employees at the Illinois

State's Attorney Office (Asbury 1950, 298). In Philadelphia, detectives arrested the "entire personnel of a police station." Later, while raiding a still they found records of a "building and loan fund" that listed the bribes being paid to police:[40]

> District captains ....$75 per month
> Detectives....................$50 per month
> Street sergeants ....$25 per month

Investigators seized bank accounts and discovered that Philadelphia police inspector John Carlin, whose annual salary from that job was around $4,000, had a bank account with $193,553.22. Inspector William McFadden's account was worth less: $102,829.45.

Meanwhile, on the other side of Pennsylvania, the election of a new mayor in Pittsburgh in 1926 caused the standard distilled beverage served in speakeasies to change from "mooney" to "administration booze," so called because it was connected with the city government. The new drink cost twice as much as the old. Customers didn't like it either, because it had an inferior taste and developed green slime if left standing for a few days. However, the desires of Pittsburgh consumers mattered little. Any seller who tried to replace administration booze with the preferred mooney was promptly raided by the police.

This is not to say that all police and enforcement agents were collecting payoffs from bootleggers. Although many local police forces had been thoroughly compromised, by the late 1920s, a large number of federal agents were honest individuals dedicated to enforcing the law. After all, they arrested tens of thousands of people and seized millions of gallons of illegal liquor.[41] But they were badly outnumbered in their fight against the millions of American "criminals" who were consuming illegal alcohol, and the incredibly ruthless, violent, well-organized criminal gangs that were supplying it.

To get an idea of what Prohibition enforcement agents were up against, consider a few cases cited in the 1931 Senate report (U.S. Congress, Senate 1931, vol. 2, 360–64):

1. Case No. 774-M: The Traum gang, which operated in the eastern Missouri/southern Indiana/southern Illinois/western Kentucky region.

In 1928, the gang of about a dozen individuals set up an office in Terre Haute, Indiana, and took control of the illegal liquor industry in the region. They operated 37 wildcat distilleries and bribed county officials for protection from the law. The organization was collecting about $13,000 per week by charging "$1.50 on every barrel of mash run off in the stills and 50 cents on every sack of sugar sold by the sugar house."

The organization owned "a number of Thompson machine guns and terrorized the community, in some instances by going to the homes of farmers, placing guns in their backs, and forcing them to put stills on their farms. . . . The deputy administrator at Indianapolis raided one of these stills and secured a confession from the farmer on whose property the still in question was located. On the following day the farmer was killed by machine gun fire as he drove through one of the main streets of Terre Haute."

2. *Case No. 175-S: The Lillian smuggling combine, which had offices in New York City and specialized in smuggling liquor from Canada and then selling it through its distribution channels.*

Employing up to 150 people, this organization purchased liquor in Canada and then loaded it onto "mother ships" with a capacity of up to 50,000 cases. The ships would sail from Canada to the international waters off the shores of Long Island and northern New Jersey, where fast, smaller boats would await word (by radio) from lookouts that the Coast Guard was not in the area. The liquor would then be offloaded from the mother ship and transported into the United States.

3. *Case No. 600-M: Conspiracy between bootleggers and government officials in Pottawatomie County, Oklahoma.*

The mayor of Earlsboro, Oklahoma, had an agreement with the county sheriff and county attorney to "protect retail liquor dealers and wholesalers . . . in their violation of the national prohibition act." The chief of police collected from $10 to $50 per week from each dealer in return for protection from the law enforcers. This arrangement went on for a number of years and was eventually "brought to the attention of the State attorney general of Oklahoma, who assigned an assistant attorney general to investigate. . . . It appears that this official also was approached and entered into the protection scheme. . . . The situation then continued until the investigation was undertaken by special agents of [the Prohibition] bureau."

4. *Case No. 762-M: The Stephens combine, which controlled the liquor production and distribution in and around San Antonio, Texas.*

After Prohibition Bureau agents raided a still outside San Antonio and took four prisoners, they realized they were onto something big when an agent guarding the prisoners was killed by another gang member in an attempt to free his comrades. The resulting investigation revealed that the Stephens organization operated 23 stills plus cutting and aging plants and controlled the liquor business in an entire section of Texas. The investigation also revealed that several state and county officials were on the payroll of the combine, which led to several indictments, including those against the assistant district attorney of Bexar County, the chief investigator of the state of Texas, and two representatives of Fleischmann's Yeast Company, which had sold the combine over $25,000 worth of yeast.

5. *Cases 596-M and 807-M: Conspiracy involving government officials in the towns of Mullan and Wallace, which are located in Shoshone County, Idaho.*

The city councils in both Mullan and Wallace set up arrangements whereby local bootleggers made regular payments to the cities "under the guise of taxes or licenses." As long as the bootleggers made their regular payments (which were used to help fund city expenses), they were allowed to operate. The resulting investigation and trials resulted in the convictions of "the sheriff and chief deputy sheriff of Shoshone County . . . and the mayor, chief of police, and entire city council of Mullan, and the mayor, former mayor, and chief of police at Wallace."

So despite the laws against alcohol production and sales, the booze flowed. It flowed because high demand existed, and the public never desired an enforcement effort of the magnitude necessary to bring about national Prohibition. The beverages were higher priced and of much lower quality than what had been available when the industry was legal, but there was plenty of it to be had at going prices. And the business was now in the hands of criminals who had completely perverted the missions of many municipal and county governments.

The Crime Wave

During the years leading up to the Eighteenth Amendment, one of the major benefits promised by Prohibition supporters was that restricting alcohol would reduce crime. Their argument revolved around the fact that people under the influence are more likely to commit various offenses, such as assault, public drunkenness, and drunk driving, and those addicted to alcohol may steal to support their drinking habit. Therefore, since Prohibition would cause alcohol consumption to fall, the crimes associated with alcohol use would decline. By extension, additional benefits would include fewer people passing through the court system and ending up in prison. Society would be better off because there would be fewer victims of crime, less property damage, and lower governmental criminal justice costs.

This prediction turned out to be highly inaccurate, and failure in this area provided major ammunition for the anti-prohibitionists. Although some categories of crimes associated with alcohol consumption declined (e.g., public drunkenness), overall crime and criminal justice costs went up, not down. There were three reasons why.

1. As already noted, the Volstead Act created millions of criminals who had not existed before: those producing, selling, or consuming alcohol in violation of the new law. Even though enforcement was spotty, hundreds of thousands of Americans were arrested for alcohol violations, and tens of thousands of them ended up in prison.

2. Because of the enhanced profit opportunities in the now-illegal alcohol trade, organized crime had a greater incentive to battle over territories of operation. Those disputes were usually settled violently, which caused the homicide rate to rise. Although most of the killings involved members of one organization murdering members of a rival group, enough innocent bystanders were hit by stray bullets or died in saloon bombings (because the saloon owner refused to serve a particular gang's beverages) that it eventually led to a public outcry over gang violence.[42]

3. Police corruption reached unprecedented levels, to the point that in some American cities, criminal gangs essentially had free reign to operate as they pleased. Not only did the illegal liquor trade flourish, so did the various other activities that criminal organizations engaged in. Prostitution and gambling are sometimes called "victimless" crimes, but protection rackets, kidnapping, and extortion are not. In some of the more lawless cities, gangs grew increasingly bolder, and as the 1920s progressed, they often carried out their operations in broad daylight on crowded streets. Widespread public resentment over criminal control of cities was another reason why Prohibition eventually lost public support.

The most violent crime is murder, and the U.S. homicide rate is shown in Figure 5.3. This measure also serves as a proxy for other violent crimes. The rate was rising before Prohibition, and that increase has been attributed in large part to the major rise in U.S. urbanization that occurred during the early 1900s from the huge influx of foreign immigrants.[43] The rate moved sharply upward in 1920, the year the Volstead Act took effect, and continued to climb during the 1920s and early 1930s. It eventually peaked at 9.7 homicides per 100,000 people in 1933, the year Prohibition ended.

The crime wave set off by national Prohibition was large enough to clog the court system and fill the jails. Although data from state and local enforcement efforts are often unavailable, numbers for federal efforts do exist. During the first 10 years of federal Prohibition enforcement, about 550,000 arrests were made on illegal alcohol charges, which led to 343,000 convictions (Lee 1963, 156–57). Many of those convictions resulted in fines, and according to Lee, total fines assessed during the first 10 years were $56,683,025.[44]

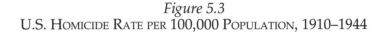

Figure 5.3
U.S. HOMICIDE RATE PER 100,000 POPULATION, 1910–1944

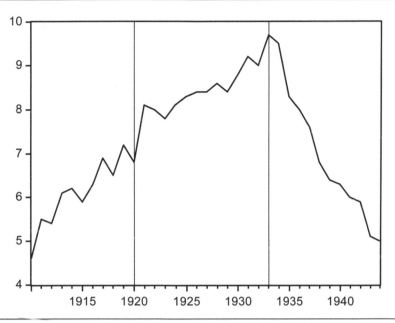

SOURCE: U.S. Department of Commerce, *Statistical Abstract of the United States,* various issues.

Prisons filled to capacity and then beyond. According to data supplied by the U.S. attorney general at the 1930 Senate hearings, from 1910 to 1929, the number of federal prisoners as a proportion of the U.S. population rose nearly sixfold, from 11.8 prisoners per 1 million people in 1910 to 64 per million by 1929 (U.S. Congress, Senate 1930, 50). Prohibition was clearly the major cause: of those 11.8 prisoners in 1910, 1.6 were incarcerated on liquor and drug charges. Of the 64 in 1929, 43 were locked up on alcohol and drug charges. Federal prisons expanded to house the increased numbers. For example, the U.S. Army turned over barracks space at Fort Leavenworth, Kansas, to enlarge the federal penitentiary there. Overcrowding led to increasingly generous paroles for convicted criminals.

In the midst of this crime wave and overload of the justice system, the prohibitionists pushed for ever-tougher penalties for alcohol violations. In 1929, the Jones Act became law, raising the maximum penalties for Volstead Act violations from six months to five years in prison and

109

raising the maximum fine from $1,000 to $10,000. Michigan went even further by making possession of alcohol a felony and passed a "four strikes and you're out law," which imposed the penalty of life imprisonment for the fourth felony conviction. Five people in Michigan were actually sentenced to life in prison for alcohol violations, one of whom was a mother with 10 children.[45]

Meanwhile, other states were going in the opposite direction. New York dropped its state enforcement law in 1923—Prohibition was never popular in that state—which meant that federal agents would have to handle the entire effort. In 1926, Montana and Wisconsin eliminated statewide enforcement, and that same year Nevada voted to repeal the Eighteenth Amendment. Illinois, Massachusetts, and Rhode Island dropped enforcement in 1930. The federal government was still enforcing Prohibition throughout the United States, but public support for the effort was slipping away.

The End of Prohibition

Anti-prohibition organizations first appeared in 1918 when the Association Against the Prohibition Amendment (AAPA) was founded. Originally funded by brewers and distillers, this group initially fought a losing battle against the tide of public opinion. However, after Americans had a few years of experience with Prohibition, public attitudes began to change, and by the mid-1920s, support was waning. Various public opinion polls were conducted, and although they used sampling methods that would be considered crude by today's standards, these polls suggested that a majority of respondents felt that the liquor laws should be changed. The fact that some states dropped their enforcement efforts during the mid-1920s is further evidence of weakening support. Interestingly, almost no one was advocating the repeal of the Eighteenth Amendment; instead the discussion was about altering the Volstead Act to allow stronger beer and wine.

The anti-prohibitionists' arguments included the following (many of which are now familiar to the reader):

1. *Prohibition had failed to make alcoholic beverages unavailable.* Anyone who wanted to purchase illegal alcohol could easily do so on the thriving black market.

2. *The alcoholic beverages that were available were often poisonous.* A huge amount of the black-market liquor was either redistilled denatured alcohol or produced by amateurs under filthy conditions.

3. *The Volstead Act had turned a nation of beer drinkers into a nation of hard liquor drinkers.* For concealment purposes, there was a shift away from high-volume beer toward considerably stronger, lower-volume distilled liquors.

4. Prohibition caused Americans to consume alcohol at younger ages. Bootleggers did not have to worry about losing a liquor license if they sold to minors. In fact, unscrupulous sellers would deal to just about anyone, including young teenagers. In addition, illegal drinking possessed an element of excitement that appealed to such a clientele.

5. It caused consumption by women to increase. Drinking in speakeasies was a trendy activity during the 1920s, and women asserted their independence by voting, smoking in public, and drinking.

6. It turned a huge proportion of the American population into criminals and in doing so promoted a general disregard for society's laws. Countless millions of Americans violated the Prohibition laws, and critics argued that this caused Americans to ignore other laws as well.

7. Prohibition caused a loss of personal freedom. As the Prohibition era went on, there were increasing complaints about enforcement methods used by the police. Search and seizure methods were criticized, as were efforts by Prohibition agents to turn Americans into informants.

8. Prohibition caused an increase in crime. There was little doubt in anyone's mind that the Volstead Act was the primary cause of the huge increase in organized crime that took place during the 1920s.

9. There was a major rise in corruption by public officials. This aspect of Prohibition was painfully clear to most Americans. Newspapers reported one scandal after another involving Prohibition, and any resident of a city like Chicago or Detroit knew that virtually the entire police force was collecting bribes from the bootleggers, or was simply too frightened to enforce the law.

10. Tax revenue was lost. Alcohol taxes had long been an important source of revenue for governments, but that revenue dried up when the business became illegal. In essence, the bootleggers earned that lost revenue. This issue was not especially important during the booming 1920s, but when the Depression took hold during the early 1930s, it became a huge concern.

11. Prohibition was bad for the U.S. economy. Before Prohibition, alcoholic beverage production employed tens of thousands of workers in distilleries, wineries, and breweries. This factor is one of the reasons why labor unions were so opposed to the prohibition of beer. Alcohol Prohibition did not abolish all of those jobs; it instead moved many of them from the legal economy to the illegal economy. The net effect on U.S. employment was negative because Prohibition raised prices, reduced quantity demanded, and caused a larger proportion of U.S. demand to be satisfied by imports.

12. It put American money into foreign hands. Since Americans were buying increased quantities of alcoholic beverages from countries like

Canada and Mexico, many argued that funds were leaving the country that would have been spent on domestic liquor if legal sources had been available.

13. *The power of the federal government increased at the expense of the states.* The Volstead Act was a federal law, enforced by federal agents, and those agents had the authority to make seizures and arrests regardless of the laws of the state they were operating in. This factor was a major issue in states that never really embraced Prohibition.

A number of prominent Americans such as Henry Joy felt so strongly about the failure of Prohibition that they were willing to donate their time and considerable financial resources to the AAPA. Another key player helping to bring about the end of Prohibition was Pierre Du Pont, the wealthy industrialist who ran the DuPont corporation along with his brothers and then later headed General Motors. Du Pont had originally supported Prohibition because he was concerned about the effects of alcohol on workers. Because his company manufactured explosives, workplace safety was a major issue at DuPont, and the company had strict rules about alcohol usage by its employees (Kyvig 1979, 80).

Like Henry Joy, Du Pont had changed his mind by the mid-1920s. One of his first clues that something was amiss was revealed to him in 1925 when U.S. Prohibition Commissioner Roy Haynes told him that, except for the city of Detroit, the United States was dry. However, managers at DuPont and GM plants had been informing Du Pont of increasing problems with employees over alcohol and bootlegging. Du Pont was bothered not only by these reports from his plants but also by the fact that the head of the U.S. Prohibition enforcement effort had so badly mischaracterized the actual situation (Kyvig 1979, 81). Du Pont did considerable reading on his own and became convinced that Prohibition had failed to restrict alcohol consumption, had encouraged lawlessness, and had been enacted in an undemocratic manner since many of the states that ratified it never put the actual question on the ballot for the voters to decide. Du Pont went on to head the Delaware chapter of the AAPA.

With wealthy, influential people like Du Pont and Joy lending their talents and money to the effort, the AAPA became an effective organization, and the anti-prohibitionist campaign gathered steam. Then in 1929, the Women's Organization for National Prohibition Reform was formed and began advocating for changes in the Prohibition laws. Within a year, it had 100,000 members (Kyvig 1979, 121). Meanwhile, the ASL was in decline. The former leadership had been replaced with new leaders who were not nearly as effective.[46]

By the early 1930s, it had become clear that a substantial majority of the U.S. public had turned against Prohibition, and a main topic of discussion was modifying the Volstead Act to allow stronger beer and wine. The more extreme step of repealing the Eighteenth Amendment was not being seriously considered because that goal was thought unattainable. Repeal would have meant adding a new amendment to the U.S. Constitution, which required the approval of 36 states. In other words, just 13 of the 48 states could have blocked the effort by refusing to ratify, an outcome that was viewed as a near certainty.

The amazing part of this story is that what seemed impossible in 1930 occurred with stunning swiftness in 1933, thereby undoing what had taken the prohibitionists decades to accomplish. It happened because the U.S. social and political situation was shaken by the Great Depression. Just as World War I greased the skids for Prohibition, the Depression helped bring about its swift end, in part because it laid waste to one of the last claims the prohibitionists could make in their favor, that banning alcohol had helped cause the economic prosperity of the 1920s. The Depression made economic conditions the major U.S. political issue during the 1932 elections. In the minds of many, U.S. economic problems and Prohibition were somehow linked, and the Democrats were able to exploit this issue by making a persuasive case that repeal would help improve business conditions.

The Depression also caused the federal budget to move into deficit. The prevailing view was that deficits should be eliminated, and that meant either raising revenue or cutting spending, or some combination of the two. A quick and obvious way to generate tax revenue was to resurrect the liquor industry. Repealing Prohibition would cause the distilleries, wineries, and breweries to once again produce in sizable amounts, and all of that legal liquor could be taxed. Revenue would flow to the U.S. Treasury, and the budget deficit would shrink. This argument was very appealing at the time and a major reason why U.S. political leaders suddenly became so interested in eliminating national Prohibition.

Reestablishing the liquor industry would also bring about another much-needed economic benefit: job creation. Thousands of workers would be hired, which would provide a much-needed stimulus to the economy. In addition, it would help U.S. farmers by increasing the demand for foodstuffs used as inputs. It would also cause Americans to purchase less imported liquor. These were sound economic arguments.

During the spring of 1932, Congress held hearings on Prohibition, and their title illustrates how the Great Depression had changed the political landscape: *Modification or Repeal of National Prohibition* (U.S. Congress, Senate 1932). Almost all of the witnesses who testified at the hearings favored either modifying the Volstead Act or repealing the Eighteenth Amendment. As the year went on and the Depression continued, the issue took on increasing importance. In addition, the candidates in the 1932 elections—especially the Democrats—were making a major issue of Prohibition repeal. The Republican platform was neither pro- nor anti-Prohibition, unlike in 1928 when it had been decidedly pro.

The Democrats won big in the 1932 elections. When Congress returned to session in January 1933, they pushed for a repeal amendment even though the Republicans still controlled Congress (the new Congress would be seated in March). Enough Republicans were willing to vote along with the Democrats that the Twenty-First Amendment passed Congress on February 20, 1933, and was sent to the states for ratification. Section 1 reads:

> The eighteenth article of amendment to the Constitution of the
> United States is hereby repealed.

Section 2 specifies that state liquor laws would prevail, and Section 3 allows the states seven years to ratify the amendment.

In March 1933, both the new Congress and President Roosevelt were sworn into office. One of Roosevelt's first moves was to issue an executive order to reduce spending on Prohibition enforcement, and then he pushed for a bill to modify the Volstead Act to allow the production and consumption of beer with 3.2 percent alcohol. That law quickly passed Congress and became effective on April 7, 1933. Meanwhile, states were ratifying the Twenty-First Amendment, and the process was completed on December 5, 1933. The Noble Experiment was over.

Modern Day Replay

There are major similarities between yesteryear's alcohol Prohibition and today's war on drugs. The United States currently spends billions of dollars each year trying to prevent its citizens from producing, importing, and consuming various narcotics. These laws are enforced by a small army of government agents and police, and this effort has helped fill our courts and prisons. The enormous profits generated by the illegal drug trade has led to corruption at various levels of government, and although it is not clear how pervasive that corruption is, it would be naive to think it is insignificant. Meanwhile, despite the enforcement effort, drugs are available to those who want to buy them. The drug laws have also caused a crime wave of epic proportions, not just in the United States but in countries like Mexico that produce and transport illegal narcotics.[47] During the past few decades, thousands of drug-related homicides have been committed in the United States. Illegal production allows modern-day criminals to mix various dangerous additives into illegal narcotics, the equivalent of the 1920s' poison booze. Medicinal marijuana is the modern version of medicinal alcohol. The similarities go on and on.

By the late 1920s, Americans had concluded that the costs of alcohol Prohibition exceeded the benefits. Recent efforts to legalize marijuana in states such as Colorado and Washington suggest that a sizable number of Americans are starting to think the same thing about laws prohibiting that substance. One wonders if they will reach the same conclusion about laws prohibiting other narcotics.[48]

6. Be Careful What You Wish For

Public dissatisfaction with social and economic conditions during the post–Civil War industrial boom led to public demands that government serve as an agent of change. This call to action resulted in a major expansion in both the scope and size of government that began in the early 20th century. Several significant policies were enacted, including the federal income tax (1913), Prohibition of alcohol (1919), and the various components of the 1930s' New Deal. Supporters of these initiatives had good intentions and genuinely believed that the policies would create positive outcomes. However, the law of unintended consequences caused results that were less positive than expected.

The goal of the federal income tax was to shift the tax burden away from the working class and toward the upper class. That outcome was accomplished, but the major unintended consequences were reducing the incentive to earn taxable income by those taxed at high rates and providing the revenue that allowed a huge expansion of the federal government. Cigarettes were taxed by the federal government, and then later by states and cities, the goal being to raise revenue. Cigarette taxes have been a large revenue source to governments, but they have also led to cigarette smuggling, a problem that has been going on for many decades and is getting worse.

The purpose of the federal minimum wage was to raise incomes of the working poor and to cause employers to replace female and child workers with adult males. This policy has had mixed results as well. Wages have been raised for low-skill workers who have jobs, but many individuals (largely teenagers) are unemployed because the minimum wage has priced them out of jobs. Alcohol Prohibition was supposed to reduce alcohol consumption, and it did so, although by nowhere near the amount supporters claimed would be the case. Meanwhile, it imposed huge costs on society in the form of poison booze, crime, and corruption.

We can expect to hear about these cases and related issues for years to come. A combination of federal government budget deficits and the growing gap between the haves and have-nots ensures that the federal income tax and the rich paying their "fair share" will continue to

117

be major topics. States are also having budgetary problems, and raising cigarette taxes is a convenient and politically expedient way to increase revenue. But every time cigarette tax rates go up, the incentive to smuggle becomes greater. With respect to the minimum wage, expect various politicians and labor union leaders to continue claiming that a higher minimum wage will make the poor better off. Alcohol Prohibition ended in 1933, but the discussion of its unintended consequences has many applications to our modern laws banning narcotics.

Meanwhile, governments pursue other policy initiatives. Two major laws were recently enacted that substantially raise the level of governmental control. The Patient Protection and Affordable Care Act (2010) increases government involvement in the health care sector, and the Dodd-Frank Wall Street Reform and Consumer Protection Act (2010) adds hundreds of new rules and regulations to the financial industry. When fully implemented, these laws will provide countless examples of the law of unintended consequences.

The primary purpose of the Patient Protection and Affordable Care Act is to expand health insurance coverage to a greater number of Americans. This law is 906 pages of single-spaced text and includes stipulations about health insurance coverage, reimbursement rules to medical providers, and new taxes to help fund the program.[1] To cite just one example of unintended consequences, the law is expected to have a negative impact on employment, especially for small companies. A major reason why is because the law imposes a tax on employers that do not provide health insurance for their employees. The tax is $2,000 per employee beginning with the 31st employee, but the employer does not pay this tax unless it employs 50 or more workers. Organizations with 49 workers are exempt.[2]

Consider a business that has 49 employees and does not provide health insurance for its workers. If it hires a 50th worker, it must either provide health care for its employees or pay the $2,000 tax. The tax does not apply to just the 50th employee, but to the number above 30. In other words, the tax would apply to a total of 20 workers, so the amount owed for hiring the 50th worker would be $40,000. This high cost makes it unlikely that the business will hire the 50th employee. In addition, businesses with more than 49 employees will have an incentive to lay off workers so they can avoid paying the tax. Another negative impact on employment concerns the fact that the law provides an incentive for employers to convert full-time workers into part-time workers. For an employee to count toward the number used to assess the tax, they must be "full-time equivalent," which is defined as working 30 hours per week. Employers can avoid the tax and having to provide health insurance for workers by keeping work-ers' hours below 30 per week.[3]

The Dodd-Frank financial reform bill also contains many opportunities for unintended consequences. This act is 848 single-spaced pages long and is designed to prevent a repeat of the financial crisis of 2007–2008.[4] One widely accepted cause of that crisis is that large financial institutions were engaging in risky activities in the mortgage market, in part because their managers and clients believed that if those financial institutions failed, the federal government would bail them out. The view was that the govern-ment would never let them fail, because doing so would cause major harm to the entire U.S. financial system. In other words, they were "too big to fail."

Dodd-Frank is designed to end "too big to fail" by requiring large finan-cial institutions to adhere to more stringent regulations, and in the event that any of them should become bankrupt, they would be liquidated un-der the Orderly Liquidation Authority without the use of taxpayer funds. However, critics of Dodd-Frank contend that rather than ending the no-tion of "too big to fail," the act institutionalizes it.[5] A reason why is because if the Orderly Liquidation Authority is not functioning properly, which is entirely possible during a financial crisis, the institutions are subject to "resolution" (i.e., bailout). In addition, by piling on more rules and regula-tions, the law makes it likely that the financial industry will become in-creasingly concentrated toward large firms. Such concentration will occur because regulations impose compliance costs on businesses, and larger organizations can spread those compliance costs over larger output, there-by reducing average cost. This factor is a common complaint about gov-ernment regulations, that they provide a competitive advantage to large firms over small firms and thus make the economy less competitive. It also explains why large firms are typically the ones claiming the need for more government regulation of their industry.[6]

These are just a few of the unintended consequences of the federal government's latest major policy initiatives. There will be many more. The lesson to be learned is that whenever government passes a new law, or imposes a new rule or regulation, there will be unintended con-sequences. Be careful what you wish for, because those unintended consequences can undo a well-intentioned government policy.

Notes

Chapter 1

[1]The U.S. homeownership rate includes second homes and vacation homes. See Haughwout, Peach, and Tracy (2010). Historical data are available at http://www.census.gov.

[2]The study by Munnell et al. is criticized by Morgenson and Rosner (2011, 32–40).

[3]Acharya et al. (2011, 36–37) note that purchases of high-risk mortgages by Fannie and Freddie slowed in the late 1990s, but picked up again in the early 2000s. Wallison (2011) reports that the two agencies were supposed to allocate 30 percent of their financing to borrowers whose incomes were at or below the median level in their community.

[4]For a detailed discussion of Fannie Mae's and Freddie Mac's roles in the mortgage debacle, see Acharya et al. (2011) or Morgenson and Rosner (2011).

[5]Normally, when discussing the law of unintended consequences, the focus is on negative effects. However, not all unintended consequences are negative. Robert Merton (1936), who is credited with being the first to provide a detailed analysis of unintended consequences, notes that Karl Marx's prediction that wealth would become increasingly concentrated in the hands of the rich led to the rise of organized labor. Merton attributes increased unionization to lessening the concentration of wealth.

[6]For examples, see Kives (2011) and Reynolds (2009). Reynolds notes that the effectiveness of traffic cameras in reducing T-bone collisions is also in doubt.

[7]See "Only and Lonely" and "Illegal Children Will Be Confiscated," *The Economist*, July 23, 2011.

Chapter 2

[1]Some states also relied heavily on a head tax, which was a tax on all adult males.

[2]There were also taxes on certain corporations' gross receipts, on interest and dividend payments by railroads, and on dividend payments by banks. During the war, approximately 10 percent of U.S. households paid federal income taxes. See Seligman (1914, 437–38).

[3]In 1867, there were about 265,000 income tax payers. The population of the northern states in the 1860 census was roughly 23 million. See Seligman (1914, 473–81). The 1861 income tax was never actually collected; the tax was altered in 1862, which is when collections began. See Witte (1985, 68).

[4]For a detailed analysis of the court case *Pollock v. Farmers' Loan and Trust Company*, see Seligman (1914, pt. 2, chap. 5).

[5]The Court also ruled that the federal government lacked the authority to tax the interest earned on bonds issued by states. See Seligman (1914, 579).

[6]The corporate income tax (1 percent on net income over $5,000) that became law in 1909 was upheld by the Supreme Court.

[7]Less than 2 percent of the U.S. labor force filed income tax returns for the 1913 tax year. See Witte (1985, 78).

[8]The income tax also greased the skids for Prohibition a few years later by reducing the federal government's dependence on alcohol taxes.

[9]The exempt income was raised to $3,500 by 1929.

[10]From 1921 to 1929, inflation-adjusted economic output in the United States rose by 48 percent, while the U.S. population rose 16 percent based on the 1920 and 1930 censuses. See R. J. Gordon (2000, A2) for the income data.

[11]Federal outlays are from *The Budget for the Fiscal Year 2010, Historical Tables*, p. 21, http://www.gpo.gov/fdsys/pkg/BUDGET-2010-TAB/pdf/BUDGET-2010-TAB.pdf.

[12]Witte (1985, chap. 5) provides details of the tax laws passed during the 1930s.

[13]Another source of revenue during the Depression was the alcohol tax after Prohibition ended in 1933.

[14]See Allen (1939, 184–88) for a discussion of wealthy Americans' disdain for Roosevelt.

[15]"Historical Highlights of the IRS," http://www.irs.gov/uac/Historical-Highlights-of-the-IRS. During 1944 and 1945, the top rate was at its all-time high of 94 percent.

[16]Aggregate U.S. output in 1945 was $214 billion.

[17]The 45 percent figure cited by Gordon covers the period from 1939 to 1946.

[18]The Medicare payroll tax is for the hospitalization insurance component. The other parts of the Medicare program do not have their own tax.

[19]"Enemies of Progress," *The Economist*, March 19–25, 2011.

[20]The Social Security tax referred to here is the OASDI tax. Wilson (2000) also reports that the bottom three deciles of income earners (where income does not include OASDI benefits) collected 49.7 percent of OASDI benefits.

[21]Another reason why these programs have expanded so rapidly is because the public's demand for them has risen more rapidly than income. In economic terms, they are "luxury goods."

[22]Recent examples of increases in federal income tax rates designed to close budget deficits occurred during the presidencies of George H. W. Bush, Bill Clinton, and Barack Obama.

[23]The Kennedy tax cuts (1964), the Reagan tax cuts (1981), and the George W. Bush tax cuts (2001) became law in years when the federal government was running budget deficits.

Chapter 3

[1]Ohio has a state liquor store system, so there are nowhere nearly as many liquor stores in that state as in Kentucky.

[2]Both Ohio and Kentucky also assess state sales tax on cigarettes, including the cigarette tax component of the price.

[3]Ohio is a major beer producer with large breweries in Columbus (Anheuser-Busch) and Trenton (Miller).

[4]The Ohio data are from http://obm.ohio.gov; the Kentucky data are from "General Fund Receipts Exceed Estimates by $83 million for FY2012," Office of the State Budget Director, Frankfort, July 12, 2012.

[5]For examples of the impact of specific states' cigarette tax increases on tax revenue, see McLean, Kahn, and Feldman (2006) for evidence from Wyoming, and Michigan Department of Treasury (2005).

[6]Incentives exist to smuggle alcohol between the two states, but the price differentials are much smaller than for cigarettes; beverages are also more expensive to transport. As a result, cigarettes are more widely smuggled.

[7]Cigarettes are also taxed heavily in Chicago through a combination of federal, state, county, and city taxes. See "Chicago May Double Cigarette Tax," *Convenience Store News*, May 27, 2009.

[8]The estimate for 2001 was $2 billion in illegal profits for U.S. smugglers. See "Where Smoke Escapes the Detectors," *Cincinnati Enquirer*, July 21, 2002. Cigarette smuggling

is also an international problem. See, for example, Merriman, Yurekli, and Chaloupka (2000) or World Health Organization (2003).

[9]This analysis assumes that the price rises by the full amount of the tax increase. Tax evasion may very easily prevent that from happening, on average, as documented here.

[10]For estimates of the price responsiveness of cigarette consumption to price changes, see Becker, Grossman, and Murphy (1994).

[11]The claim that reducing cigarette consumption lowers health care costs is debatable. Lower tobacco consumption reduces health care costs associated with respiratory problems, but it also causes people to live longer, which raises health care costs.

[12]This was not the first tax on tobacco in the United States. Alexander Hamilton attempted to have a tax imposed in 1794 to help provide revenue for the new government of the United States. Ultimately, the tax applied only to snuff, and it was short-lived.

[13]The federal government's fiscal year runs from July 1 to June 30. Data are taken from U.S. Bureau of the Census (1975, 1108).

[14]See Burns (2007, esp. chap. 8), for a discussion of the tobacco prohibition effort.

[15]New York City's cigarette tax expired in 1940, but the smuggling continued because of New York's state tax. Then, when the city had budget problems again in the early 1950s, it reinstituted the 1-cent tax. By this time, the state was charging 3 cents, so the total tax for city residents was 4 cents per pack.

[16]See Orzechowski and Walker (2007, 9–10) for a historical listing of state cigarette tax rates.

[17]The plan was never passed by the New York legislature because upstate lawmakers did not want to subsidize New York City. See Fleenor (2003, 9–10).

[18]To see why inflation reduces the tax differential, consider the following example. If one state's tax is $1.00 per pack of cigarettes while another state's tax is $0.10, the differential is $0.90. A 5 percent inflation reduces the inflation-adjusted tax in the first state to $0.95, and to $0.095 in the second state. The inflation-adjusted tax differential is now $0.855.

[19]In over-the-road smuggling, the cigarette purchases are being reported to the state taxing agency in the low-tax state, but the cigarettes are then sold in a high-tax state with counterfeit stamps on the packs.

[20]A U.S. government official told the author (off the record) that these cigarettes are most likely to be sold in rural areas and at convenience store–gas stations located along interstate highways.

[21]Exports are exempt from domestic taxes because to do otherwise could place the domestic producer at a disadvantage against foreign competitors.

[22]"States Go to War on Cigarette Smuggling," *Wall Street Journal*, July 20, 2009.

[23]Data on the proportion of adults who smoke are available from the Centers for Disease Control, Behavioral Risk Factor Surveillance System, http://www.cdc.gov/brfss/. Per capita taxed cigarette sales are taken from Orzechowski and Walker (2007, 39–40).

[24]Indian reservation sales are discussed in more detail below. The existence of Indian reservations in Washington is believed to be a major reason why that state's taxed cigarette sales are so low. See Stehr (2005, 285).

[25]For examples of statistical estimates, see Fleenor (1998) and Thursby and Thursby (2000).

[26]Fleenor (1998) reports that a small proportion of nonsmuggled cigarettes (0.5 percent) were purchased in Mexico and carried across the U.S. border.

[27]Studies with estimates of cigarette smuggling and cross-border shopping include Saba et al. (1995), Coats (1995), Fleenor (1998), Thursby and Thursby (2000), Stehr (2005), Lovenheim (2008), and LaFaive, Fleenor, and Nesbit (2008).

[28]See "Suits Claim Wide Reach of Cigarettes from Tribes," *New York Times*, October 2, 2008; and "'Cig Break' Brawl," *New York Post*, April 27, 2008. An investigation by Marina Walker Guevara and Kate Willson of the Center for Public Integrity contends that a large proportion of those cigarettes were sold to smugglers and documents their delivery sites on the reservation as being signs on a post. See Guevara and Willson, "Big Tobacco's New York Black Market: How America's Top Cigarette Firms Fueled a Billion-Dollar Underground Trade," Center for Public Integrity, Washington, December 19, 2008.

[29]"State Drops Collection of Taxes on Indian Cigarettes," *Buffalo News*, August 15, 2009.

[30]"'Cig Break' Brawl," *New York Post*, April 27, 2008.

[31]Orzechowski and Walker (2007, 34).

[32]Buffalo Creek Treaty, May 20, 1842, article ninth.

[33]For the Seneca's description of the events during 1997, see "April 22: Seneca Nation Update" (http://sisis.nativeweb.org/seneca/apr22up.html) and "Letter from Seneca President Mark Schindler to US President Bill Clinton" (http://sisis.nativeweb.org/seneca/apr27sch.html).

[34]"Senecas Seek U.S. Troops to Ward Off Cigarette Taxes," *Reuters*, January 13, 2009.

[35]Tom Hays, "EU Accuses R. J. Reynolds of Smuggling Cigarettes, Laundering Money," Associated Press, November 1, 2002.

[36]See "U.S. Authorities Bust Cigarette-Smuggling Ring Linked to Hezbollah," CNN. com, July 21, 2000, and "Cigarette Smuggling Linked to Terrorism," *Washington Post*, June 8, 2004.

[37]See U.S. General Accounting Office (1997) for a description of what happened in Canada. One U.S. state that has gone against the trend is New Hampshire, which in 2011 reduced its cigarette tax by 10 cents per pack.

Chapter 4

[1]This is the federal minimum wage in 2013.

[2]See Ryan (1920), who was an early 20th-century advocate of the living wage.

[3]Additional arguments used at this time for the minimum wage were that it would make women more likely to fulfill their duties as mothers and would also make women less likely to become prostitutes. See Leonard (2005).

[4]National Industrial Conference Board (1927, 14).

[5]See Hall and Ferguson (1998) for an analysis of the causes and consequences of the Great Depression.

[6]See Chandler (1970, 229–37) for a discussion of the trade practices under the NIRA.

[7]See Paulsen (1996) for a discussion of the political machinations that led to the wage and work rules specified in the NIRA.

[8]The NIRA was declared unconstitutional because the Supreme Court said the federal government did not have the right to regulate intrastate commerce (trade taking place within a state). See Shlaes (2007, esp. chap. 8) for an entertaining discussion of the legal battle against the NIRA.

[9]The patterns in Figures 4.1 and 4.2 also appear in the data for females.

[10]Williams also notes that minimum wage laws were an important component of the South African apartheid laws. The discussion that follows helps explain why the series plotted in these figures have stayed high.

[11]The three increases were legislated in 2007 near the end of the economic boom. Congress and the White House could have canceled the 2008 and 2009 increases once it became clear the economy was in the grips of the Great Recession.

[12]See Neumark and Wascher (2006) for a survey of these studies. They conclude that a 10 percent increase in the minimum wage causes a decline in teenage employment of 1–3 percent.

[13]In 2005, about half of those earning the minimum wage were between the ages of 16 and 24. See "Time for the Minimum Wage to Punch Out?" *Wall Street Journal*, November 11–12, 2006. See also Levin-Waldman (2001, 29), who notes that "earners of the minimum wage are for the most part teenagers or contributing members to a household budget."

[14]See Neumark and Wascher (2006, 24–25).

[15]See Phillips (1981) for an example of a study that suggests a relationship between increases in the minimum wage and crime.

Chapter 5

[1]Letter from Henry Joy to Thomas H. Brennan, Deputy Prohibition Commissioner at Detroit, March 11, 1927, Henry B. Joy Papers, Bentley Historical Library, Ann Arbor, MI.

[2]"Joy Quits Club as Dry Protest," *Detroit News*, December 15, 1929.

[3]Telegram from Henry Joy to President Calvin Coolidge, January 10, 1927, Henry B. Joy Papers, Bentley Historical Library, Ann Arbor, MI.

[4]Letter from Henry Joy to Andrew Mellon, March 12, 1928, Henry B. Joy Papers, Bentley Historical Library, Ann Arbor, MI.

[5]Coffee eventually became a popular drink that could compete on price with whiskey, but that did not occur until the late 1820s.

[6]Corn prices in the West were lower enough than in the East—even after netting out transportation costs—that western whiskey was cheaper than whiskey produced in the East from eastern corn. According to Rorabaugh (1979, 79), by the early 1800s western corn prices of 25 cents per bushel allowed distillers to convert corn into whiskey, which could then be sold in the East for four times that amount after transportation costs.

[7]When the U.S. federal government was formed in 1789, Treasury Secretary Alexander Hamilton pushed for a tax on distilled spirits as a way to generate much-needed revenue for the new government. By this time, western whiskey had replaced eastern rum as the major distilled beverage produced in North America, so the burden of the tax fell on the westerners. It was this distilled-liquor tax that led to the 1794 Whiskey Rebellion in western Pennsylvania, which required federal troops to quell it. The excise tax was dropped in 1802.

[8]Apparently, the first religious figure in North America to argue that alcohol was evil was the Reverend Francis Makenzie, who did so in 1705. See Cherrington (1920, 32).

[9]A barrel holds 31 gallons. Output data are taken from *Brewers Almanac 1944* (New York: United States Brewers Foundation, 1944), 36–37.

[10]Eventually, every state except Rhode Island and Connecticut ratified the Eighteenth Amendment.

[11]The pro-beer forces entered into the record the results from various medical experiments and testimonials from a number of people claiming that it was impossible for a person to drink enough low-alcohol beer to get drunk. The ASL provided evidence purporting to show the opposite. For the pro-beer evidence, see U.S. Congress, Senate (1919, 265–313); for the anti-beer evidence, see U.S. Congress, Senate (1919, 72–77, 313–16, 328–40).

[12]Gompers's idea of emphasizing education programs made sense because informing the public of the evils of excessive drinking would reduce the demand for alcohol. Prohibition was trying to reduce consumption by restricting supply.

[13]Denaturation is the process of adding chemicals to grain alcohol to make it unfit for human consumption.

[14]One reason why the 0.5 percent alcohol content was allowed was because a few witnesses and senators pointed out at the hearings that various beverages (buttermilk, root beer, and apple cider) contain low levels of alcohol.

[15]During the first few years of U.S. Prohibition, many of these customs forms identified the United States as the point of destination. That changed in the mid-1920s

when Canada agreed to stop exporting to the United States. But all that change meant was that the customs forms could no longer identify the United States as the destination point. Finally, in the early 1930s, the United States leaned hard enough on the Canadians that Canada made it illegal to export alcoholic beverages to the United States.

[16]Canada imposed various forms of Prohibition at the provincial level but never adopted it as wholeheartedly as the United States did. See Brown (1994, esp. chap. 5).

[17]Considerable smuggling also occurred at the U.S.-Canadian border via trucks, automobiles, and railroads.

[18]Payment schemes from smugglers to border agents are described in Association Against the Prohibition Amendment (1929, 16–17). It estimates that the total graft paid to border patrol agents in the Detroit was $2 million per year, which amounts to an average of about $1,700 per border patrol employee.

[19]This system was set up under the 1897 Bottled-in-Bond Act. Distilleries would produce "straight whiskey" without any additives and then place it inside a bonded warehouse for aging. When the alcohol was withdrawn from the warehouse, a per-gallon tax was paid by the whiskey owner to the federal government.

[20]These warehouses held an additional 4.7 million gallons of rum, gin, and brandy, plus 2.5 million gallons of nonbeverage alcohol.

[21]See "Medicine," Time, July 29, 1929. In 1920, witnesses testified before Congress that there was enough bonded whiskey to satisfy medicinal demand for 30–50 years. See U.S. Congress, House (1920, 36).

[22]See Lindsay (1974) for a description of Remus's bootlegging operation.

[23]The standard whiskey barrel holds 42 gallons of liquid.

[24]This information came out at the trial. Remus turned state's evidence and testified against his fellow criminals in order to avoid a long jail sentence.

[25]"Fabulous George Remus Dies; Made Millions as Bootleg King." Cincinnati Enquirer, January 21, 1952.

[26]See Bergreen (1994, 130–34) for a description of the Genna brothers' operation.

[27]Various denaturing formulas were necessary because the addition of a particular chemical could make the alcohol fit for one industrial use but unfit for others.

[28]Haynes (1923, 186) reports the same number from Prohibition Unit tests of seized liquor during the early 1920s.

[29]Kobler (1973, 309) claims 11,700 deaths from alcohol in 1927 alone, but it is unclear where he obtained that number. Haynes (1923, 186) reports that during the first six months of 1923, 100 people died in Chicago from drinking tainted liquor, and another 600 in Philadelphia from alcohol (tainted and otherwise). The federal government maintained statistics on deaths from wood alcohol poisoning, and those deaths numbered a few hundred each year (see Feldman [1930, 401]). Statistics on alcohol-related deaths caused by "alcoholism" and "cirrhosis of the liver" were maintained (more on this later), but many observers think that these figures mix together people who died from consumption of "clean" alcohol and those poisoned by tainted liquor. Of course, in many cases both factors played a role in their deaths.

[30]See, for example, Feldman (1930).

[31]Warburton's estimates have been largely confirmed using more modern statistical techniques. See Miron and Zwiebel (1991).

[32]Wickersham Report (1931, 216).

[33]Yet another series that reinforces these results is hospital admissions and discharges for alcoholism. See Warburton (1932, 216).

[34]The fact that health problems stemming from heavy alcohol consumption declined so much during and immediately after World War I is discussed by Dills and Miron (2004). They contend that Prohibition's effect may be overstated because World War I

(1917–1918) and the flu pandemic (1918) significantly raised death rates, especially for young adult males who are the ones most likely to drink heavily and die of alcohol-related diseases. Since there were fewer young adult males by the early 1920s, the alcohol death rate would have dropped independent of the law.

[35]These data are for the end of fiscal year 1920 and are taken from U.S. Congress, Senate (1931, vol. 2, 208).

[36]Typical annual earnings for an unskilled manufacturing worker in a U.S. city at that time were about $1,200–$1,500 per year, whereas a skilled worker earned $2,000–$2,500.

[37]Federal spending data are from U.S. Department of Commerce (1966, 170), which gives total government spending in 1929 as $8.48 billion. To determine the federal share, the data for 1929 shown on page 173 were used to determine that federal spending was 16 percent of total government spending during that year. Thus, $1.36 billion equals 0.16 × $8.48 billion.

[38]The 1931 Senate report (vol. 2, pt. I) donates an entire chapter (17) to this problem.

[39]See Manderville (1925) about Detroit and Kobler (1973, 234) about New York.

[40]Data in this section are from Association Against the Prohibition Amendment (1929, 6–7).

[41]Just during fiscal years 1929 and 1930, federal agents made over 68,000 arrests for Prohibition violations. See U.S. Congress, Senate (1931 vol. 2, 357).

[42]Miron (1999) argues that Prohibition enforcement could actually raise the crime rate by upsetting the existing black-market arrangements between gangs and setting off a fight to establish a new order.

[43]Miron (1999) says that another reason why the homicide rate rose during the Prohibition era was because the proportion of young adult males in the US population increased.

[44]By the late 1920s, the federal courts were so clogged with cases that prosecutors routinely offered plea bargains in an attempt to speed the cases through the system.

[45]These five people did not serve life terms because the Michigan legislature later reduced the penalty—but they did spend several years in jail.

[46]The head of the ASL during the late 1920s was Bishop James Cannon Jr. Among other things, he was exposed as being a gambler and hoarder of foodstuffs during World War I. See Asbury (1950, 322).

[47]Not surprisingly, in an effort to reduce drug violence in their countries, several Latin American leaders have called on the United States to legalize various drugs. See, for example, "Mexico Drug Violence Shows Decline," *Wall Street Journal*, June 14, 2012.

[48]Obviously, the issue of eliminating laws that prohibit addictive narcotics has no easy answer. For an interesting discussion, see Kleiman, Caulkins, and Hawken (2011).

Chapter 6

[1]http://www.gpo.gov/fdsys/pkg/BILLS-111hr3590enr/pdf/BILLS-111hr3590enr.pdf.

[2]An employee is defined as a full-time equivalent, which is a person working 30 hours per week. Two employees working 15 hours per week also constitute one full-time equivalent employee.

[3]See "ObamaCare and the '20ers,'" *Wall Street Journal*, February 22, 2013. For another unintended consequence of the law, see "Employers Eye Bare-Bones Health Plans under New Law," *Wall Street Journal*, May 20, 2013.

[4]http://www.sec.gov/about/laws/wallstreetreform-cpa.pdf.

[5]See Statement of Joshua Rosner, Managing Director, Graham Fisher & Co., before the House Committee on Financial Services Subcommittee on Oversight and Investigations, "Who Is Too Big to Fail: Does Title II of the Dodd-Frank Act Enshrine Taxpayer Funded

Bailouts?" May 14, 2013, http://www.scribd.com/doc/141572927/Rosner-Testimony-on-Title-II-05-14-2013.

[6]See Skeel (2011) for a detailed discussion of the unintended consequences of the Dodd-Frank legislation.

References

Acharya, Viral V., Matthew Richardson, Stijn Van Nieuwerburgh, and Lawrence J. White. 2011. *Guaranteed to Fail: Fannie Mae, Freddie Mac and the Debacle of Mortgage Finance.* Princeton, NJ: Princeton University Press.

Allen, Frederick Lewis. 1939. *Since Yesterday: The Nineteen-Thirties in America, September 3, 1929–September 3, 1939.* New York: Harper Brothers.

Asbury, Herbert. 1950. *The Great Illusion: An Informal History of Prohibition.* Garden City, NJ: Doubleday.

Association Against the Prohibition Amendment. 1929. *Scandals of Prohibition Enforcement.* Washington: National Press Building.

Bader, Robert Smith. 1986. *Prohibition in Kansas: A History.* Lawrence: University of Kansas Press.

Becker, Gary S., Michael Grossman, and Kevin M. Murphy. 1994. "An Empirical Analysis of Cigarette Addiction." *American Economic Review* 84 (3): 396–418.

Bergreen, Laurence. 1994. *Capone: The Man and the Era.* New York: Touchstone.

Bettmann, Otto L. 1974. *The Good Old Days: They Were Terrible!* New York: Random House.

Billingslea, William. 2004. "Illicit Cigarette Trafficking and the Funding of Terrorism." *Police Chief*, February, pp. 49–54.

Boardman, Barrington. 1988. *"Typhoid Mary" and the Bomb: An Anecdotal History of the United States from 1923–1945.* New York: Harper & Row.

Brown, Lorraine. 1994. *The Story of Canadian Whiskey.* Markham, Ontario: Fitzhenry & Whiteside.

Brownlee, W. Elliot. 1996. *Federal Taxation in America: A Short History.* Cambridge: Cambridge University Press.

Burns, Eric. 2007. *The Smoke of the Gods: A Social History of Tobacco.* Philadelphia: Temple University Press.

Carson, Gerald. 1977. *The Golden Egg: The Personal Income Tax: Where It Came From, How It Grew.* Boston: Houghton Mifflin.

Case, Karl E., and Robert J. Shiller. 2003. "Is There a Bubble in the Housing Market?" *Brookings Papers on Economic Activity* 34 (2): 299–362.

Chandler, Lester. 1970. *America's Greatest Depression: 1929–1941.* New York: Harper & Row.

Cherrington, Ernest H. 1920. *The Evolution of Prohibition in the United States of America: A Chronological History of the Liquor Problem and the Temperance Reform in the United States from the Earliest Settlements to the Consummation of National Prohibition.* Westerville, OH: American Issue Press.

Coats, R. Morris. 1995. "A Note on Estimating Cross-Border Effects of State Cigarette Taxes." *National Tax Journal* 48 (4): 573–84.

Council of Economic Advisers. Various issues. *Economic Report of the President.* Washington: Government Printing Office.

Dills, Angela K., and Jeffrey A. Miron. 2004. "Alcohol Prohibition and Cirrhosis." *American Law and Economics Review* 6 (2): 285–318.

Even, William, and David Macpherson. 2010. "Teen Employment Crisis: The Effects of the 2007–2009 Federal Minimum Wage Increases on Teen Employment." Employment Policies Institute, Washington.

Faulkner, Harold Underwood. 1960. *American Economic History*. 8th ed. New York: Harper & Row.

Feldman, Herman. 1930. *Prohibition: Its Economic and Industrial Aspects*. New York: Appleton.

Fleenor, Patrick. 1998. "How Excise Tax Differentials Affect Interstate Smuggling and Cross-Border Sales of Cigarettes in the United States." Background Paper no. 26, Tax Foundation, Washington.

———. 2003. "Cigarette Taxes, Black Markets, and Crime: Lessons from New York's 50-Year Losing Battle." Cato Institute Policy Analysis no. 468, February 6.

———. 2008. "Cigarette Taxes Are Fueling Organized Crime." *Wall Street Journal*, May 7.

Gallo, Ernest, and Julio Gallo. 1994. *Ernest and Julio Gallo: Our Story*. New York: Times Books.

Gordon, Robert A. 1974. *Economic Instability and Growth: The American Record*. New York: Harper & Row.

Gordon, Robert J. 2000. *Macroeconomics*. 8th ed. Boston: Addison-Wesley.

Hall, Thomas E., and J. David Ferguson. 1998. *The Great Depression: An International Disaster of Perverse Economic Policies*. Ann Arbor: University of Michigan Press.

Haughwout, Andrew, Richard Peach, and Joseph Tracy. 2010. "The Homeownership Gap." Federal Reserve Bank of New York *Current Issues in Economics and Finance* 16 (5): 1–10.

Haynes, Roy A. 1923. *Prohibition Inside Out*. Garden City, NJ: Doubleday, Page.

Holian, Timothy J. 2000. *Over the Barrel: The Brewing History and Beer Culture of Cincinnati*. Vol. 1, *1800 – Prohibition*. St. Joseph, MO: Sudhaus Press.

Josephson, Matthew. 1934. *The Robber Barons*. New York: Harcourt, Brace.

Kives, Bartley. 2011. "Cameras Cut T-Bone Crashes." *Winnipeg Free Press*, July 6.

Kleiman, Mark A. R., Jonathan P. Caulkins, and Angela Hawken. 2011. *Drugs and Drug Policy: What Everyone Needs to Know*. Oxford: Oxford University Press.

Kobler, John. 1973. *Ardent Spirits: The Rise and Fall of Prohibition*. New York: G. P. Putnam's Sons.

Kyvig, David E. 1979. *Repealing National Prohibition*. Chicago: University of Chicago Press.

LaFaive, Michael, Patrick Fleenor, and Todd Nesbit. 2008. *Cigarette Taxes and Smuggling: A Statistical Analysis and Historical Review*. Midland, MI: Mackinac Center for Public Policy.

Lakins, Nekisha E., Robin A. LaVallee, Gerald D. Williams, and Hsiao-ye Yi. 2007. "Apparent per Capita Alcohol Consumption: National, State, and Regional Trends, 1977–2005." Surveillance Report no. 82, National Institute on Alcohol Abuse and Alcoholism, Bethesda, MD.

Lee, Henry. 1963. *How Dry We Were: Prohibition Revisited*. Englewood Cliffs, NJ: Prentice-Hall.

Leonard, Thomas C. 2005. "Protecting Family and Race: The Progressive Case for Regulating Wages." *American Journal of Economics and Sociology* 64 (3): 757–91.

Levin-Waldman, Oren M. 2001. *The Case of the Minimum Wage: Competing Policy Models*. Albany: State University of New York Press.

Lindsay, Thomas J. 1974. "George Remus: Big Daddy of the Bootleggers." *Cincinnati*, vol. 8, no. 2, pp. 8–12.

Lovenheim, Michael F. 2008. "How Far to the Border? The Extent and Impact of Cross-Border Casual Cigarette Smuggling." *National Tax Journal* 61 (1): 7–33.

Manderville, Ernest W. 1925. "Detroit Sets a Bad Example." *Outlook*, August 22. [Reprinted in *The Twenties: Fords, Flappers, and Fanatics*, ed. George E. Mowry. Englewood Cliffs, NJ: Prentice-Hall, 1963.]

McLean, Marcus, Zafar Dad Khan, and Laura Feldman. 2006. "Impact of the 2003 Cigarette Excise Tax Increase on Consumption and Revenue in the State of Wyoming: Second Quarterly Report." Wyoming Survey and Analysis Center, University of Wyoming, Laramie.

Merriman, David, Ayda Yurekli, and Frank J. Chaloupka. 2000. "How Big Is the Worldwide Cigarette Smuggling Problem?" In *Tobacco Control in Developing Countries*, ed. Prabhat Jha and Frank Chaloupka. Oxford: Oxford University Press.

Merton, Robert K. 1936. "The Unanticipated Consequences of Social Action." *American Sociological Review* 1 (6): 894–904.

Michigan Department of Treasury. 2005. "Michigan's Cigarette and Tobacco Taxes, 2004." Tax Analysis Division, Bureau of Tax and Economic Policy, Lansing.

Miron, Jeffrey A. 1999. "Violence and the U.S. Prohibitions of Drugs and Alcohol." *American Law and Economics Review* 1 (1): 78–114.

Miron, Jeffrey A., and Jeffrey Zwiebel. 1991. "Alcohol Consumption during Prohibition." *American Economic Review* 81 (2): 242–47.

Moore, Stephen, and Richard Vedder. 2010. "Higher Taxes Won't Reduce the Deficit." *Wall Street Journal*, November 22.

Morgenson, Gretchen, and Joshua Rosner. 2011. *Reckles$ Endangerment: How Outsized Ambition, Greed, and Corruption Led to Economic Armageddon*. New York: Times Books

Munnell, Alicia, Lynn E. Browne, James McEneaney, and Geoffrey M. B. Tootell. 1992. "Mortgage Lending in Boston: Interpreting HMDA Data." Working Paper no. 92-7, Federal Reserve Bank of Boston.

National Industrial Conference Board. 1927. *Minimum Wage Legislation in Massachusetts*. New York: National Industrial Conference Board.

Neumark, David, and William Wascher. 1992. "Employment Effects of Minimum and Subminimum Wages: Panel Data on State Minimum Wage Laws." *Industrial and Labor Relations Review* 46 (1): 55–81.

———. 2006. "Minimum Wages and Employment: A Review of Evidence from the New Minimum Wage Research." Working Paper no. 12663, National Bureau of Economic Research, Cambridge, MA.

Nie, Weiliang. 2010. "China's One-Child Policy: Success or Failure?" BBC News Asia-Pacific, September 24.

Nordlund, Willis J. 1997. *The Quest for a Living Wage: The History of the Federal Minimum Wage Program*. Westport, CT: Greenwood Press.

Orzechowski and Walker. 2007. *The Tax Burden on Tobacco: Historical Compilation*. Arlington, VA: Orzechowski and Walker.

Paulsen, George E. 1996. *A Living Wage for the Forgotten Man: The Quest for Fair Labor Standards, 1933–1941*. Selinsgrove, PA: Susquehanna University Press.

Phillips, Llad. 1981. "Some Aspects of the Social Pathological Behavioral Effects of Unemployment among Young People." In *The Economics of Legal Minimum Wages*, ed. Simon Rottenberg. Washington: American Enterprise Institute for Public Policy Research.

Plavchan, Ronald Jan. 1976. *A History of Anheuser-Busch, 1852–1933*. New York: Arno.

Reynolds, Glenn Harlan. 2009. "Stoplight Traffic Cameras: Why Is Big Brother Ticketing You?" *Popular Mechanics*, October 1.

Robert, Joseph C. 1949. *The Story of Tobacco in America*. New York: Alfred A. Knopf.

Rorabaugh, W. J. 1979. *The Alcoholic Republic*. New York: Oxford University Press.

Ryan, John A. 1920. *A Living Wage*. Revised and abridged version. New York: MacMillan Company.

Saba, Richard P., T. Randolph Beard, Robert B. Ekelund Jr., and Rand W. Ressler. 1995. "The Demand for Cigarette Smuggling." *Economic Inquiry* 33 (2): 189–202.

Seligman, Edwin R. A. 1914. *The Income Tax: A Study of the History, Theory and Practice of Income Taxation at Home and Abroad*. 2nd ed., revised and enlarged. New York: MacMillan. [Reprints of Economic Classics. New York: Augustus M. Kelley Publishers, 1970.]

Shlaes, Amity. 2007. *The Forgotten Man: A New History of the Great Depression*. New York: HarperCollins.

Skeel, David. 2011. *The New Financial Deal: Understanding the Dodd-Frank Act and Its (Unintended) Consequences*. Hoboken, NJ: John Wiley.

Smith, Adam. (1776) 1993. *An Inquiry into the Nature and Causes of the Wealth of Nations*. Oxford: Oxford University Press.

Stehr, Mark. 2005. "Cigarette Tax Avoidance and Evasion." *Journal of Health Economics* 24 (2): 277–97.

Steuerle, C. Eugene, and Stephanie Rennane. 2011. "Social Security and Medicare Taxes and Benefits over a Lifetime." Urban Institute, Washington.

Thursby, Jerry G., and Marie C. Thursby. 2000. "Interstate Cigarette Bootlegging: Extent, Revenue Losses, and Effects of Federal Intervention." *National Tax Journal* 53 (1): 59–77.

U.S. Bureau of the Census. 1975. *Historical Statistics of the United States: Colonial Times to 1970*. Bicentennial Edition, Part 2. Washington: Government Printing Office.

U.S. Congress. House. Committee on Ways and Means. 1920. *Hearings on Safeguarding of Liquor in Bonded Warehouses*, Parts 1 and 2. February 25 and December 17.

———. House. Subcommittee of the Committee on Ways and Means. 1927. *Hearings on Enforcement of Customs, Narcotic, and Prohibition Laws*. February 21 and 24.

U.S. Congress. Senate. Subcommittee on the Judiciary. 1919. *Hearings on Prohibiting Intoxicating Beverages*. 66th Cong. 1st Sess.

———. 1930. *Investigation of Prohibition Enforcement: Hearings before the Committee on the Judiciary*. 71st Cong., 2nd sess., Part 2, April 7.

———. 1931. *Enforcement of the Prohibition Laws: Official Records of the National Commission on Law Observance and Enforcement in Five Volumes*. 71st Cong., 3rd sess.1.

———. Senate. Subcommittee of the Committee on the Judiciary. 1932. *Hearings on Modification or Repeal of National Prohibition*. April 14–15, 19–21, and May 17.

U.S. Department of Commerce. 1966. *Long Term Economic Growth 1860–1965*. Washington: Government Printing Office.

———. Various issues. *Statistical Abstract of the United States*. Washington: Government Printing Office.

U.S. Department of Labor, Bureau of Labor Standards. 1967. *Minimum Wage Legislation*. Washington: U.S. Department of Labor.

———. 1975. *Handbook of Labor Statistics 1975*. Reference ed. Washington: Government Printing Office.

U.S. General Accounting Office. 1997. *Cigarette Smuggling: Interstate and U.S.-Canadian Experience*. Statement of Robert A. Robinson, Director, Food and Agricultural Issues, Resources, Community, and Economic Development Division before the House Subcommittee on Health and Environment of the Committee on Commerce, December 9.

———. 2003. *Terrorist Financing: U.S. Agencies Should Systematically Assess Terrorists' Use of Alternative Funding Mechanisms*. Report to Congressional Requesters, November.

Vedder, Richard K. 1997. "Bordering on Chaos: Fiscal Federalism and Excise Taxes." In *Taxing Choice: The Predatory Politics of Fiscal Discrimination*, ed. William F. Shughart II. Oakland, CA: Independent Institute.

Velde, Francois R. 2009. "The Recession of 1937: A Cautionary Tale." Federal Reserve Bank of Chicago *Economic Perspectives* 33 (4th quarter): 16–35.

Wallison, Peter J. 2011. "Wall Street's Gullible Occupiers." *Wall Street Journal*, October 12.

Warburton, Clark. 1932. *The Economic Results of Prohibition*. New York: Columbia University Press.

Wickersham Report. 1931. *Report on the Enforcement of the Prohibition Laws of the United States*. Washington: U.S. National Commission on Law Observance and Enforcement, January 7.

Williams, Walter. 2010a. "Minimum Wage Cruelty." *Cincinnati Enquirer*, April 18.

———. 2010b. "Minimum Wage Is a Proven Job Killer." *Cincinnati Enquirer*, May 30.

Wilson, D. Mark. 2000. "Who Pays the Payroll Tax? Understanding the Tax and Income Dynamics of the Social Security Program." No. CDA00-03, Heritage Center for Data Analysis, Washington.

Witte, John F. 1985. *The Politics and Development of the Federal Income Tax.* Madison: University of Wisconsin Press.

World Health Organization. 2003. "The Cigarette 'Transit' Road to the Islamic Republic of Iran and Iraq: Illicit Tobacco Trade in the Middle East." Regional Office for the Eastern Mediterranean, Cairo.

Index

Note for index: Following a page number, an *f* indicates a figure, an *n* indicates a note, and a *t* indicates a table.

Afghanistan, funding of terrorist training camps, 48
alcohol
  additives to alcohol, 84, 85
  arrests for drunkenness, 100, 101*f*
  consumption in 1710–1840, 72*t*–73
  consumption, early movement against excessive, 73–75
  consumption by minors, 49, 76, 79, 81, 111
  consumption by women, 69–70, 111
  deaths from, 100, 126*n*29, 126*n*34–127*n*34
  denatured, 85, 93, 97, 98, 100
  excise tax on, 9, 10, 11
  industrial, 85–86, 97–98
  medicinal, 69, 77, 86, 92–95
  quality concerns, 84, 85, 87–88
  wood, 97–98, 126*n*29
alcohol Prohibition, 7, 67–115. *See also* alcohol Prohibition, enforcement
  Anti-Saloon League, 79–81, 83, 84, 86, 103, 125*n*11, 127*n*46
  beer. *See* beer.
  bonded warehouses, 92–95
  bootlegging, 69, 85, 88, 92–95, 94, 103, 107
  consumption during, 98–101, 99*f*
  and corruption and bribery, 88, 92, 96, 102, 103–4, 108
  and crime, 69, 79, 88–89, 104, 107–10
  and crime, organized, 104–7
  demand, methods for supplying, 89–98
  enactment, changing views after, 67–69
  end of, 110–14
  fines and jail terms, 86, 108–10
  and immigrants, 75–76, 87
  and law of unintended consequences, 7, 69, 87–88, 117

  moonshining, 89, 95–98
  near beer, 86, 96
  problem, inherent with, 86–89
  saloon problem, 79–81
  smuggling, 67, 89, 91–92, 106
  speakeasies, 69–70, 95–96, 100, 105
  temperance societies, 74, 75, 79–81
  underage drinking, 79
  war on drugs, similarity to, 114–15
  women and prohibition movement, 76–77, 112
  and World War I, 82, 83
alcohol Prohibition, enforcement, 81, 83, 87, 92
  and corruption, 88, 92, 96, 102, 103–4, 105, 108
  costs of, 85, 88–89, 101–2, 103–4
  and Henry Joy, 66–67
  and organized crime, 104–7
  by state and local government, 103–4
alcohol taxes, 111
American Federation of Labor, 84
American Temperance Society, 74
Anheuser-Busch, 76, 78, 82, 122*n*3
Anti-Saloon League (ASL), 79–81, 83, 84, 86, 103, 125*n*11, 127*n*46
Asbury, Herbert, 96–97
Association Against the Prohibition Amendment (AAPA), 110–11

beer
  alcohol content of, 76
  consumption statistics in 1710–1840, 72*t*
  and end of Prohibition, 110, 112
  and Prohibition, 82, 88
black market. *See also* moonshining
  for alcohol, 93, 94–95, 110
  for cigarettes, 49
black teenagers and employment, 59, 60*f*, 61*f*
bonded warehouses, 92–95

135

About the Author

Thomas E. Hall is a professor of economics at Miami University in Oxford, Ohio, where he teaches classes on macroeconomics, business cycles, and the Great Depression. He received his BA from the University of Colorado and his MA and PhD degrees from the University of California – Santa Barbara. He has written articles in applied macroeconomics and is the author of several books, including *Business Cycles: The Nature and Causes of Economic Fluctuations; The Great Depression: An International Disaster of Perverse Economic Policies* (with J.D. Ferguson); *The Rotten Fruits of Economic Controls and the Rise From the Ashes, 1965-1989.*

Cato Institute

Founded in 1977, the Cato Institute is a public policy research foundation dedicated to broadening the parameters of policy debate to allow consideration of more options that are consistent with the principles of limited government, individual liberty, and peace. To that end, the Institute strives to achieve greater involvement of the intelligent, concerned lay public in questions of policy and the proper role of government.

The Institute is named for Cato's Letters, libertarian pamphlets that were widely read in the American Colonies in the early 18th century and played a major role in laying the philosophical foundation for the American Revolution.

Despite the achievement of the nation's Founders, today virtually no aspect of life is free from government encroachment. A pervasive intolerance for individual rights is shown by government's arbitrary intrusions into private economic transactions and its disregard for civil liberties. And while freedom around the globe has notably increased in the past several decades, many countries have moved in the opposite direction, and most governments still do not respect or safeguard the wide range of civil and economic liberties.

To address those issues, the Cato Institute undertakes an extensive publications program on the complete spectrum of policy issues. Books, monographs, and shorter studies are commissioned to examine the federal budget, Social Security, regulation, military spending, international trade, and myriad other issues. Major policy conferences are held throughout the year, from which papers are published thrice yearly in the Cato Journal. The Institute also publishes the quarterly magazine Regulation.

In order to maintain its independence, the Cato Institute accepts no government funding. Contributions are received from foundations, corporations, and individuals, and other revenue is generated from the sale of publications. The Institute is a nonprofit, tax-exempt, educational foundation under Section 501(c)3 of the Internal Revenue Code.

CATO INSTITUTE
1000 Massachusetts Ave., N.W.
Washington, D.C. 20001
www.cato.org